An OPUS book

POLICING LIBERAL SOCIETY

Policing Liberal Society

STEVE UGLOW

Oxford   New York

OXFORD UNIVERSITY PRESS

1988

Oxford University Press, Walton Street, Oxford OX2 6DP

Oxford New York Toronto
Delhi Bombay Calcutta Madras Karachi
Petaling Jaya Singapore Hong Kong Tokyo
Nairobi Dar es Salaam Cape Town
Melbourne Auckland

and associated companies in
Beirut Berlin Ibadan Nicosia

Oxford is a trade mark of Oxford University Press

British Library Cataloguing in Publication Data
Uglow, Steve
Policing liberal society.—(OPUS)
1. Police—Great Britain
I. Title II. Series
363.2'0941 HV8195. A2
ISBN 0-19-219222-1
ISBN 0-19-289218-5 Pbk

Library of Congress Cataloging in Publication Data
Uglow, Steve.
Policing liberal society / Steve Uglow.
p. cm.—(An OPUS book)
Bibliography: p.
Includes index.
1. Police—Great Britain. 2. Law enforcement—Great Britain.
I. Title. II. Series: OPUS.
HV8195.A2U36 1988
363.2'0941—dc19 87-28729
ISBN 0-19-219222-1
ISBN 0-19-289218-5 (pbk.)

Set by Colset Pte Ltd, Singapore
Printed in Great Britain by
Biddles Ltd.
Guildford and King's Lynn

In memory of Police Constable Lewin Uglow
For Olive and Phil

Preface

When I started teaching a course on the police in the mid-1970s there was a dearth of literature on the subject. Over the past ten years that gap has been filled by reports and inquiries, by research studies, by journalism, and by several academic books. Historians, lawyers, sociologists, newspapermen—all have contributed. Not the least valuable have been the studies commissioned by the Metropolitan Police themselves through the Policy Studies Institute.

Why another? The excellent works that have appeared are mainly specialist and detailed, while the general studies are often too complacent. I felt that there was a need for a book which would inform the reader about police development and organization and the central facets of police work, but was also a critical overview of policing. Policing is too often assumed to be the answer to the problems of crime and social control. We are too willing to allow the police extra resources and powers so long as they promise us salvation from the twin evils of crime and disorder. It is a theme of this book that we are mistaken, both about the nature of these 'evils' and in our belief that the police can materially affect the situation. Furthermore, we take serious risks in not recognizing the changes in the constitutional balance between individual and state that the changes in policing are bringing about.

This is not an anti-police book, although I feel that they have gained a status and power beyond that needed for an emergency public service. We need the police service just as we need health and education services. But it angers me that in this country nurses, social workers, and teachers should often be better qualified, better trained, doing equally important jobs, often facing similar dangers, but infinitely worse paid and worse equipped. We have our priorities wrong about our public services and, as I shall argue, the police often do not regard themselves as a public service at all.

I owe a debt of gratitude to many writers, as will appear in the text and bibliography. Also to many colleagues (especially in the Law

Department and particularly Richard de Friend) at the University of Kent, whose stimulating and aggravating ideas have laid some of the groundwork for this book. Thanks to Ron, who kept me company throughout the writing of this book and whose cheerfulness and common sense were a wonderful antidote. Thanks to Joyce, without whom I can say this book would never have emerged. But the true moving spirit behind all this, providing intellectual stimulus, emotional support, and sheer hard work in reading, criticizing, and subbing, is Jenny.

Contents

1

The Job

Introduction

We all recognize contrasting, even contradictory, images of the police—the officer on the beat courteously directing tourists; the patrol car, blue light flashing, speeding in pursuit of a stolen vehicle; massed ranks of policemen clad in helmets, wielding truncheons, confronting demonstrators or strikers; officers talking to school-children about road safety or the dangers of glue-sniffing; Special Branch officers tapping telephones or opening mail; incident rooms co-ordinating house-to-house enquiries; the village bobby pushing a bicycle and chatting to customers at the local shop.

All these are part of our everyday idea of the police, although we absorb them at second hand, from fiction, documentaries, or news items. On the whole we take them for granted, although we are in fact enduring a level of police interference in private lives that earlier, unpoliced societies would have found intolerable. The police presence reaches into the family, the school, the workplace, as well as onto the streets. We grant the police massive public resources, over £3 billion a year, and wide-ranging powers. Yet we persist in seeing ourselves merely as a 'policed society' underpinned by the traditional liberal values of individual freedom, and contrast ourselves comfortably with the 'police states' of Eastern Europe or South Africa. The comfort lies in our assumption that there are well-established boundaries to policing in Britain, very different to those totalitarian regimes where the police are presumed to have wide and arbitrary powers of interference in the lives of citizens, whether Russian dissidents or South African schoolchildren. Here, we believe, there is a 'constitutional' quality to policing and this resolves any anxieties about its pervasiveness or expense.

What do we understand by 'constitutional' policing? This

question is the subject of this book. How real and how secure are the constraints placed on the British police? What does the job of policing consist of, that we may know its boundaries? Is there a 'proper' manner of policing? From where does a police force derive 'authority' so that we regard its exercise of power as legitimate? Such questions are central to any analysis and understanding.

Most occupations have a core of activity—teachers teach, doctors heal, plumbers plumb. For a constable there is no service which can be clearly labelled 'police work'—indeed, to 'police' a situation can mean involvement in and control over every minute aspect. The difficulty that confronts us in defining the core of the occupation also means that its boundaries are obscure—for other professionals, involving themselves outside the proper sphere of their work invites the response 'It's not your business'. There is very little that is not police business.

Etymologically the word 'police' is derived from the Greek 'polis', the city, but its meaning has encompassed all aspects of the government of a city and its inhabitants. (This breadth of function is shown in Greek or Roman society where the regulation of the market-place was a major 'police' function.) Similarly, in Britain in the eighteenth century the political economist Adam Smith used the term as synonymous with local government, and the narrower definition, which concentrated on the enforcement of the criminal law, only developed during the latter half of that century: from 1748 the Fielding brothers were magistrates at Bow Street and created the 'Runners' as an embryonic police force; in 1785 William Pitt's abortive Police Bill was the forerunner of many legislative attempts at reform; in 1797 Patrick Colquhoun, another magistrate, set up the Dock police and wrote on the 'new science of the police'. By the mid-nineteenth century it had become a term for a body of men rather than any clearly defined function. Policing was what 'the police' did.

But while the breadth and tasks of policing are far from self-evident, modern debate concentrates not so much on the jobs undertaken by the police as on the manner of their performance. Different concerns affect this relationship between the police and the public. First, is the question how far the police are integrated into the local community rather than being seen as external and imposed upon it: and related to this, how much reliance is put on physical force rather than unarmed persuasion. Secondly, there is a constant dilemma whether the police should operate in a restricted 'fire-brigading' fashion (coming when called) or should adopt a more preventive role, taking the initiative in monitoring activities and individuals. A third concern is the extent of a force's independence: they may set their own standards and be accountable only to the law; they may be subject to political control and required to adhere to the demands made by the government; or there may be some other form of democratic control.

Integration, reaction, independence—these factors vary to produce different types and different perceptions of police forces, although they may be performing the same basic job. Western European forces tend to be subject to much stricter political and judicial control and to be regarded as a lower-status occupation than the British force does. As with the substantive tasks of policing, the manner of operation (whether minimalist or para-military) is not inherent in the job. Are certain characteristics and methods appropriate in a liberal, democratic society and to what extent do our police forces possess and exercise them?

So the debates surrounding policing raise issues concerning the content and style of the job. But why do we accept control over our lives and regard it as 'proper' or 'legitimate' interference? Content and style certainly affect that perception—with other public occupations, the key factor for public acceptance is often the effective provision of services, such as health or education. But how do we test whether our policing services are being adequately or correctly provided? We are concerned about the service (there is constant anxiety about rising crime) and about the manner of policing (there is increasing public demand for foot patrols). But beyond these are further issues surrounding their acceptability—the police represent a general social authority and we are concerned with the limitations imposed not merely on their legal powers but on their power in general. Their own recognition of constraints over their power contributes as much to the public acceptance of police authority as do any limits on the tasks they undertake or on the manner in which they are performed.

Constraints come from different sources: legal limits; political conventions against direct government interference; local organizations to prevent the development of a 'state' police; budgetary and technical restraints to control the extent of penetration of civil society. These are critical restrictions on an otherwise open-ended police task—limits which are in favour of the liberty of the subject; and however substantial or insubstantial these constraints may be, they provide a guideline for an assessment of the 'propriety' of police action.

There is a second, more positive, side to a community's acceptance of policing and this is adherence not merely to the law but to general principles of fairness—among others the neutral and universal application of the law. Restraint and fairness are two significant factors in the general acceptability or legitimacy of the police and are touchstones of the constitutional quality in British policing. But the safeguarding of these has ramifications beyond the police, largely because of their symbolic role. According to its fundamental tenets, a liberal society should interfere in individuals' lives only when this is wholly necessary and according to the precepts of the rule of law. In police actions we can see, undisguised, the boundary markers of state interference and these should embody cherished constitutional values, especially the control of power and the primacy of the individual.

The 'bobby' has been a potent and peculiarly evocative symbol of these values. The elements of timelessness and continuity, especially in the anachronistic uniform and ancient pushbike, reflect the constancy and natural order of the 'rule of law' itself. The lack of firearms places the constable on an equal plane with the individual citizen, emphasizing the voluntary and consensual nature of the relationship between citizen and state. Thus the social-control task of the police is not seen as external imposition or naked aggression. This image confirms for us certain attributes about our social order and its political and constitutional system. In a society without a written constitution and without entrenched civil rights, the importance of such symbols cannot be underestimated. However, their form and meaning has undergone a transformation.

The Tasks of Policing

This transformation becomes clear if we look in more detail at the tasks, modes of operation, and legitimacy of the police. All these aspects of their work will receive more attention in later chapters, but a first step might be to outline the day-to-day content of the job—the routine physical tasks. At once these turn out to be complex, even contradictory, for the police officer can be seen as crimefighter, bureaucrat, crowd controller, intelligence officer, and social worker simultaneously.

The image of 'crimefighter' is the one which dominates public perception and is also strongly adhered to within the force. We believe that the primary service the police offer is the ability to 'do something' about crime and crime rates. However, the relationship between criminal behaviour and the police is more subtle, as will be explained in Chapter 4, and the commonplace that policing is about the 'detection and prevention of crime' requires exploration. In fact, police work is mainly reactive, responding to demands from the public which not only discovers and reports offences but usually provides the solution. Increases in personnel and reorganization, new procedures and technological innovations, seem to have little effect on the incidence of crime. The protection from crime provided by the police is less than might be supposed, and it might be useful to see their role more as that of a symbolic deterrent and a promise of security for the community.

The ethos of 'crimefighting' is cherished, as it has importance both politically for government and institutionally for the police. But in fact police capacity to affect crime rates is inevitably marginal—for the public the chief importance of the police lies more in their ability to provide assistance in a wide range of difficult situations.

A second crime-related function is the controlling and defusing of disputes. Many crimes resemble private disputes which become public property when the police are called in. Their very presence and status are often enough to ensure that the dispute is settled, be it between a husband and wife in a scene of domestic violence, drivers after an accident, or a restaurant manager and a disgruntled customer. Officers have a range of techniques at their disposal, not necessarily simply criminal definitions (though their power to mobilize the full force of the law encourages acquiescence). These non-legal techniques include non-intervention, conciliation, compensation, and therapy. Called to a 'domestic', the constable might act as a marriage guidance counsellor or he might just decide that this was not police business and walk away, despite clear evidence of, say, assault. At the scene of a road accident, by judicious apportionment of blame, he might persuade the drivers to settle through their insurance companies. In the restaurant, he might ensure that the bill got paid but with deductions to take account of the customer's complaints, almost acting as a small claims court allocating damages. Finally, the drunk or the mentally handicapped or the homeless might be directed towards detoxification centres or the social services.

While criminal charges may not be brought, the policeman's homily is often present, especially when cautioning juveniles. The stressing of the importance of abiding by the rules, the conjuring up of a sense of shame and guilt, lessons in good neighbouring or parenthood, all these make police officers more than merely the negotiators of the situation, outsiders with common sense and a threat of force. They become the weavers of moral tales, maintaining and reinforcing a sense of social order and of social place, of authority and deference.

This process is not necessarily subtle, and often the aim is informal punishment through humiliation and the threat of violence: 'Why don't you try it on me? If that had been my old lady I'd have knocked seven different kinds of it out of you and you'd have trouble snatching a purse again, wouldn't you? You'd better give it up or one day you'll come across a bloke like me . . .'[1]

Just as crimefighting is overestimated, so the bureaucratic and administrative aspects of police work are underestimated. 'Paper-pushing' is seen as an inevitable but despised adjunct to 'real' police work. But the station is the focus of police activity—even officers allocated to patrol duties spend between 30 and 40 per cent of their time there. Crime-related work is only a small percentage of this—perhaps as little as 2 per cent of uniformed officers' time is occupied in interviewing suspects and taking statements. Outside the station there is a similar pattern, with around 15 per cent of patrol time taken up in dealing with incidents. Even the Criminal Investigation Department (CID) is desk-bound, with 30 per cent of its time spent on investigations, a further third taken up with the paperwork which follows crime reports, and the rest spent on desultory duties including court attendance, car and person checks, training, and even—astonishingly—school-crossing relief.

Recently the paperwork has increased as a result of the Police and Criminal Evidence Act 1984 which places officers under a new statutory duty to make written records of encounters with the public—for example, while there is an enhanced power to stop and search persons and vehicles, the officer is required to make a record of such a search as soon as is practical. Furthermore, there are new custody officers at police stations, whose duties include keeping a written record of a suspect's time in custody.

Although with the creation of the Crown Prosecution Service in 1986 the police are no longer responsible for prosecutions, collecting statements and other evidence for a contested trial will take on average two weeks of an officer's time, and the time spent on form-filling will actually represent at least a quarter of the total hours spent on any cleared-up offence.

Both custody records and the preparations for a trial are immediately related to crime. But other administrative tasks include the supervision of a broad and disparate range of people and activities— the registration of aliens, the licensing of firearms, public houses, clubs, street traders, charity collectors, betting shops, taxis, and many more.

A third major function is the maintenance of 'public order'. The management of public space and public enterprise—roads, crowds, inns—is very much police business. The police are judged on the quality of 'order' in public life. Whereas access to the private world is gained through formal and precise criteria (search warrants, for instance), these are not applicable in public spaces. But although privacy appears to constrain police action, the character of the actor often determines whether an act is vulnerable through its public quality or immune by reason of its privacy: the young, working-class, black male can rely only to a limited extent on his right to privacy whereas the middle-aged, middle-class, white woman tends to be treated with deference both on the street and in her home.

In public activity of any sort the police can take a 'legitimate' interest, disregarding the hurdles of private rights. Officers can stop and search, move on gangs of youths, drunks, vagrants, shut down street traders, or turn a blind eye to buskers—irritants to many, especially to established shopkeepers. Chief Constables treat patrolling as the central police function and the beat officer as the front line of the force. This is somewhat ironic, as most crime is committed in private. Public crime, such as pickpocketing or street fighting, forms only a small proportion of the whole, but the very fact of police visibility is thought to reassure the community.

An increasingly important aspect of public order is the control of crowds, whether at football matches, political demonstrations, or industrial disputes, and this, as we shall see in Chapter 5, is one of the most controversial types of police activity and one of the areas most sensitive to government pressure. Rights to freedom of assembly and demonstration, to free speech and a free press, were recognized as important political gains in the seventeenth and eighteenth centuries, but the emergence in the nineteenth century of an urban working class with political ambitions led to public conflicts. The working class presented a threat to established order by the use of the very freedoms that the bourgeoisie had fought so hard to win. Even nowadays 'crowd control' is not a neutral management technique but has inevitable political overtones.

A similar area, where policing has strong links with central government, is the surveillance of the population mounted by the police and the security services. This will be explored in detail in Chapter 6: with its techniques for collecting all sorts of intelligence on private citizens it is the function that casts most doubt on our image of the police because it highlights their relationship with the state and the lack of restraints on police action. The constitutional basis of policing, the neutrality, independence, and accountability of the force are thrown into question and the police are seen as acting directly in support of the government.

At almost the opposite pole is the function least considered to be a central part of police work: social work. Yet this turns out to be one of the most important, for the police are the one body who provide a flexible and immediate response to problems and have the manpower and expertise to deal with situations that most citizens find difficult or impossible to handle. In flood or snow it is the police who co-ordinate relief services. In disasters, such as the capsizing of the *Herald of Free Enterprise* in March 1987, the Kent police headquarters was the information hub for distressed relatives and friends. On a less dramatic level, it transpires that about 60 per cent of the telephone calls received in a police station are related not to crime but to personal enquiries and difficulties: missing persons, lost property, people locked out of their houses. In emergencies the police deliver messages, goods, and sometimes babies. They are also an important source of information about other agencies which may provide help—a women's refuge, a drug clinic, or the WRVS. They deal with petty nuisances, drunks, minor disputes, requests for directions. The road accident is the archetype—first on the scene, the police must provide first aid and comfort, order the traffic, clean up the mess, give messages and comfort to relatives. And all of this regardless of whether any criminal offence has been committed.

Although there are other organizations and government departments for long-term problems, a quick and skilful response is needed to deal with the unexpected short-term crises which face individuals or the community. The police provide this without our even noticing it—nor (unlike the social services) do they shut down at night or over the weekend.

This outline of police jobs shows the difficulty of defining the boundaries of 'real' policing. The police have a complex relationship with the law, with the State, and with the community. None of these relationships is easy to define, yet they all make their different demands concerning the tasks that a police force should perform. But any discussion of policing must also cover the manner in which these tasks are carried out.

The Tactics of Policing

The 'mode' of policing can vary enormously in different societies. There are perhaps four elements which need consideration and on which this study will concentrate: the extent to which the police are integrated into the community (or conversely are imposed upon it); the availability and use of physical force; the way the police can be reactive (that is, passively responding to public demand) or pro-active, both in crime control and in surveillance; and, finally, the degree of independence in their relationship with local and national government. These elements directly affect a society's experience of its police and are as important as the jobs they perform.

Integration finds expression in the idea of 'community policing' which, as advocated by John Alderson while he was Chief Constable of Devon and Cornwall, at root conceives of the constable as significantly integrated into the community, knowing his parishioners, taking part in community life, and acting as conciliator and therapist, while using penal powers of arrest and force as a last resource. The demand for more foot patrols has led to several experiments, not merely in rural areas but also in Brixton and Handsworth: this is often said to indicate a return to a traditional golden age of policing.

This mythical golden age is normally contrasted with the 'confrontational' approach of the present day, particularly in public-order work but also in operations such as SWAMP '81 where the Metropolitan force, faced with the problem of street crime in Brixton, concentrated large numbers of officers in one area and, by wide-scale stops, searches, arrests, and prosecutions, sought to intimidate and deter what was seen as a criminal and dangerous section of the population. The operation is often cited as a direct cause of the riots of that year.

Thus the police can appear either as an invading army or as integrated within the community. Modern policing is a compound of the two: Lord Scarman, in his report on the Brixton riots, argues that debate about the mode of policing cannot simply contrast a hard militaristic style to a softer community-based option. Police tactics require imagination and flexibility so that the response can vary according to the needs.

But are the two extremes of para-militarism and community policing compatible approaches within a single institution? Even the appearance of integration is hard enough for the police to achieve—the force has distinct personnel, entrance rituals, dress, procedures, a stock of professional knowledge, occupational values, and attitudes. Like the law or the Church, it is clearly separate from the everyday world. Yet the police are an inevitable part of that world, perceived as an integral element in the civilized state for the day-to-day maintenance of social order. Such contradictions are ever-present—policemen and policewomen are the embodiment of the 'rule of law', yet their actions and decisions are clearly those of human beings, subject to discussion and criticism. Uniform, housing, training, attitudes—all tend to separate the officer from the rest of society. Set aside from the community yet continuously involved, police officers, like priests, can never take off the uniform. To do so seems underhand—the nineteenth-century reluctance to accept plain-clothes detectives, 'spies', is mirrored today. True integration is not possible—whether on a bicycle or in a Panda car, on Special Branch surveillance or on concentrated deployment in a particular community, policing is always an extraneous imposition on everyday life.

Yet there is a continuous and subtle process of persuasion that it is not imposed on society but forms a natural part of it: '. . . the unarmed friendly constable helping the aged . . . the young and those in distress; the determined yet scrupulous pursuer of the offender; the neutral protector of life and property, using a minimum of violence and intelligent crime prevention techniques in the "public interest"! All these are the dominant images of our time.'[2]

These images, and phrases such as 'policing by consent' and 'community policing', form the language of persuasion. Of course, without the consent of the public it is no longer policing but repression. That we do closely identify with 'our' police is shown by the high degree of approval for and co-operation with them. But this esteem to some extent derives from the favourable attitude of the media and entertainment industries, since knowledge about the police is, for most people, gleaned at second-hand. Our 'consent' is at root artificial, constrained by the limitations of our knowledge.

These paradoxes—integration yet separation, mingled satisfaction and hostility behind a façade of consent—are still present in community policing schemes, which play down the coercive and penal aspects of the job and stress the officer's interaction with the neighbourhood. Yet at bottom such schemes do not change the intrinsic relationship between the people and the officer, who still remains part of a hierarchical and disciplined force. Would it be practicable for officers to be recruited by, controlled by, and accountable to the communities in which they operate? At present there is no scheme for such a radical change. The village policeman may work in the village but he still owes allegiance to headquarters.

Modern policing is imposed authority, whether its style is paramilitary or community. The 'flexibility and imagination' of which Scarman speaks can make that imposition more palatable. The police are not immune from the pressures of public opinion, but the influence and interests of the State ultimately predominate. They would, however, be seriously flawed in public estimation were they clearly seen to be 'state police'. On a continuum between integration and imposition, the theory of 'proper' policing tends strongly to the former, eschewing violence and stressing local involvement. England has long been unique in giving significant priority to this image. But although the government and senior officers continue to use the language of integration and co-operation, we should not forget that the police have drastically developed their capacity to operate as a 'third force', trained, armed, and easily deployed to confront strikes, protests, and demonstrations.

The threshold at which physical force is used by the police makes certain constitutional realities explicit. The State has delegated to the police the right to use force in civil society—no other violence is regarded as legitimate. Even the use of troops, a regular occurrence in strikes before the First World War, is now inevitably politically sensitive. The capacity to use force crystallizes the relationship between individual and state, defining the measure of control that citizens are granted over their own lives. An arbitrary, unpredictable, or high level of violence affects the beliefs held by the citizen about the self-determination of the individual and about the constitutional relationship. The guiding principle developed within liberal societies has been that such force must be *essential* and *minimum*. The former implies that state violence is a tactic of last resort, the latter that the violence must be no more than is needed to prevent the anticipated harm. The unarmed police officer has always been an important symbol of this principle.

But recent governments have shown greater willingness to intervene and to use considerable force in industrial and political conflict—a tendency which will be discussed in more detail in Chapter 3. This puts at risk the image of the police as personifying neutrality, balance, and independence. Precisely because they are a significant part of the ideology of the rule of law, they must use physical violence sparingly and with discretion if they are to retain credibility.

The historical lesson of the early nineteenth century was that military force exacerbated rather than reduced disorder: General Napier, confronting the Chartists in 1839, saw the development of provincial police forces as the alternative to civil war—social control was to be clothed in the acceptable constitutional garb of the police uniform, and this approach, with its implicit democratic ethos, worked to encourage the co-option of the working class into the changing political and economic structures, in tandem with their increasing political enfranchisement.

The past decade has seen this process go into reverse. There has been a substantial increase in weapon-training, in the issue of firearms, and in the acceptance of these methods by the officers. Although the British force is still seen as unarmed and commonly adopts low-profile approaches (sitting out a siege or withdrawing from confrontation), there is a contradiction between the unarmed image and the well-armed and well-trained reality—a contradiction that the public has recently begun to recognize and question.

If one were to ask what has brought this change about, the police would point to the riots of 1981 as well as to an increase in armed crime. But is this a justifiable argument? Prior to those events, 'criminal' violence was rarely a problem—England remains remarkably stable and non-violent. The problems of armed crime, terrorism, or public order have never been such as to require a drastic reorientation. A better explanation is that the transformation of the British police into an armed force did not result from any immediate domestic problem but reflected developments in other parts of the world (although Northern Ireland, Baader-Meinhof, or the Red Army Faction presented very different issues to those in the United Kingdom). But the fear of such developments in Britain does not explain the scale of the alteration.

Another, more likely, cause is the social and political polarization of Britain in the 1980s and the recognition that industrial and political stability would be hard to maintain at a time of continuing high unemployment throughout Western Europe. It was in response to such fears (parallel, as we shall see, to those in the early years of the nineteenth-century police) that the change came about from the passive, non-interventionist role of the post-war years to the more dramatic pro-active and pre-emptive role of today.

There have been other departures from the traditional reactive role. Normally the police have responded to calls from the public or to events arising on patrol. But, as we shall see in Chapter 3, the increasing development of squads to investigate specific areas (robbery, prostitution, obscene publications, drugs, political 'subversion') shows a new direction, a movement towards initiating investigations, targeting their own areas of concern. With management techniques such as these the police define their objectives in different terms to those suggested by the lower profile of the community policeman. The rationale for the reorganization is the greater efficiency of such squads, bringing together resources and skilled personnel to concentrate on particular problems. The danger is that the specialist squad takes a narrow view of the police job: arrests and convictions spell success. This can have a detrimental effect on both the immediate and the longer-term objectives in the relationship between the police and the community.

Pro-active policing has many practical costs to be weighed against speculative gains in the reduction of crime. There are further questions to be asked about the principle of pro-active policing—a principle which would justify police involvement to prevent and deter

offences. This again raises the problem of the boundaries of legitimate police action. From the standpoint of traditional liberal analysis, only the commission of an offence (or its immediate threat) should
justify active intervention. One of my recurring themes will be that
the police should be reactive: while they may, almost incidentally,
prevent and deter crime, they should see their primary job as
responding to the demands made on them by the public. Above all
they should not be regarded, or regard themselves, as social engin-
eers, however benevolent.

The final important factor in defining the style and perception of
policing in any country is the extent of the force's dependence on the
State. In Britain the numerous early forces—except for the Metropolitan Police—were decentralized and lacked formal links with
central government. With local control exercised through Watch
Committees, state influence was kept to a minimum. In the mid-
nineteenth century this structure both allayed the anxieties of the
middle classes about national police forces on the French model and
maintained the tradition of local government.

But, as we shall see in Chapter 3, the balance of power has shifted
since the Police Act 1964. The powers of the chief officers have
increased, and although their relationship with the Home Office is
still one of technical independence the influence of the government
has become more obvious. Since 1974 machinery (known as the
National Reporting Centre) has been available for co-ordinating
police actions on a national basis. Yet the image of the police still
persists as locally based and significantly independent. The 'local'
quality stresses integration and implies that local police know the
'best interests' of their community. The element of independence
suggests that the force is unaffected by the influences of economic or
political groupings and owes allegiance only to an abstraction, the
rule of law. Yet again this image misrepresents the reality. Constitutionally the police occupy an anomalous (and extraordinary) position
when compared to other public agencies. There are no direct lines of
accountability between the police and the executive, legislature,
or judiciary. Unlike the heads of the health or education services
Chief Constables are independent and autocratic—as Ben Whitaker
has put it, England and Wales are governed 'not by 1 queen but by 43
kings'. This remarkable autonomy, set alongside the decline of local
control and the rise of national executive influence, has meant that

Britain has evolved a system of policing unlike any other in Western Europe.

The Legitimacy of Policing

Tasks and tactics are two of the elements of the policing equation. A third, as noted above, is acceptance that the force is exercising a legitimate power—that is, that the legal and physical powers of intervention are being used in a 'proper' manner. This depends partly on the tasks performed by the police, partly on the mode of performance, and partly on adherence to the principles not just of law but also of fairness.

Modern policing is regarded as an acceptable and legitimate form of social control. But this had to be fought for. The new form of policing developed in the nineteenth century was strenuously opposed—the Birmingham Chartists on 25 November 1839 resolved at a joint meeting with the Quakers 'to have no police whatsoever until the working classes had a voice in the making of the laws of the land'. Trust in the police grew throughout the Victorian era, but the acceptance of their authority always remained contingent on their 'good behaviour', especially in working-class districts.

It is still the case that the police work 'on probation'. This is shown by the change of emphasis on policing priorities over the past fifteen years. Until 1982 under Metropolitan Police Commissioners Mark and McNee, stress was placed on the police's capacity to provide law-and-order services, especially the 'war against crime'. A failure to deliver the goods despite substantial resources was the start of a 'crisis of legitimacy' for the police. This deepened with the inner-city riots, which were clearly labelled 'anti-police' and a reaction to aggressive policing, especially in the black communities. Commissioners Newman and Imbert have sought to re-establish legitimacy by strengthening public involvement through Neighbourhood Watch schemes, more consultative committees, and a more flexible, multi-agency approach. This policy also informs the Metropolitan Police's *Principles of Policing*, produced in 1985 and suggesting relegitimation through policing style. At the same time, greater public awareness of the limits of the police's capacity to affect crime rates has resulted in a lower profile on crime control.

But legitimacy does not depend solely on these factors—the

assumption of a democratic state is that executive functions are subject to the overarching concept of the 'rule of law'. Civil servants and politicians as well as the police are accountable for their actions and decisions, not only to political processes but to a body of doctrine that is in theory wholly separate and unsullied by those processes. The idea of the 'rule of law' underpins liberal thinking on the freedom of the individual in relation to the state. Conformity to the rule of law is a major factor in the legitimacy of state action in general but is even more important for the police since they stand directly between the citizen and the State. That they are seen to operate within the constitutional constraints of the 'rule of law', not to bend the rules or cut corners, becomes a major criterion for assessing policing. The judgement is complicated still further since the police do not merely base their actions on law but are perceived as (and behave as if they are) integral to and representative of the law itself. Acceptance of the authority of the police is directly linked to acceptance of the authority of the law.

But there is a further problem, since police functions and powers are not spelled out in clear-cut legal rules but are inevitably discretionary. 'Proper' policing requires the police to conform not to straightforward statutory provisions but, more important, to broad standards that recent jurisprudence would call 'fairness'. As will be discussed in Chapter 8, 'fairness' means that underlying standards of procedural or formal justice must be observed. These ideals, 'natural justice', imply certain institutional and operational consequences for the police.

First, they imply a level of independence for the command structure of the police who should not operate as a private army for sectional interests. Secondly, they require police action to be taken on the basis of legally defensible criteria, difficult to specify but including the avoidance of arbitrary and prejudiced acts, sensitivity to the rights of individuals, and indifference to the racial, political or ethnic character of those affected. Finally, adherence to the 'rule of law' should impose the constraints on 'open-ended' policing discussed above, ensuring that police intervention is mainly reactive and occurs only on the basis of reasonable belief that a breach of the law or of the peace has occurred or is imminent.

When senior officers refer to police accountability to the rule of law, what they have in mind is not these basic standards of fairness but the possibility of review by legal action taken by aggrieved individuals. But concern about the boundaries of 'proper' policing should not be so easily deflected: the propriety of policing is an amalgam of the tasks performed, the manner in which they are performed, and the standards of legality and fairness of the whole.

Policing, then, is not just crimefighting, social work, or social sanitation. The job description of a police officer is difficult enough to write, but is obscured by two other factors. The first is ideological. The police may exist as much in the public imagination as they do in reality—they are a central symbol within our social order. Struggle over the control and function of the police in the political arena is inevitable: the attempts by metropolitan councils in the 1980s to influence the policing of the police was one of the factors that brought them into conflict with central government and led to their abolition. The debate over community policing is as much about social relationships and the balance between authoritarian and democratic forms of social control as it is about crime. The issue is 'whose police force is it?', not 'what does it do?'

The ideological significance of the police for political groupings is one obstacle to analysis of their function. But there are also the paradoxes inherent in the job—the police possess and use physical force yet are equally expected to operate in a social-assistance role: it is difficult for them to dwell in both camps, ready to help old ladies across the street but prepared to inflict fatal violence on other citizens. A further paradox is implicit in the conflict between autonomy on the one hand and genuflection to government policy on the other. The police are mobilized by the government to break strikes and to control demonstrations, but the definition of the police as 'state functionaries, necessary for the reproduction of capitalist social relations, protecting the property of the capitalist and securing certain of the conditions of labour discipline'[3] is too limited, as it is for the law itself.

The police have institutional habits, interests, and inertias of their own. They also exist in a complex relationship with the community, the press, politicians, and civil servants. But while the power of these groups varies, there is an underlying congruence of view and of interest, especially between senior police officers, the Home Office, and governments. Although police autonomy appears circumscribed, this cosy relationship makes outside constraints scarcely visible. The fundamental issue in any discussion of a police force is its relationship with the State, and this will be explored in the following chapters.

2

The Origins of the Police

The Prehistory

Different ages have seen different forms of social control. In Britain, the development of the police in the nineteenth century was a radical departure, although it spread all over the globe in the following 150 years. It was radical in that the force did not merely represent the physical might of the sovereign or dominant class in order to coerce the population or operate as a spy network. The 'New Police', though organized along military lines of command, were officers with individual responsibility, employed to patrol the everyday life of the community in a non-aggressive manner and regulated by law.

Unpoliced societies were and are capable of self-regulation without such a public agency. Anglo-Saxon society had little that could be seen as 'public' law-enforcement—the mobilization of the law and the courts depended on the initiative of private citizens who were usually seeking not public benefit but personal compensation. To modern eyes, the award of money damages for harm done to some private interest is a tort system, not criminal justice. Before the Norman Conquest it was backed up by ties of kinship and the ultimate right to wreak vengeance through the blood feud. The communal interest was represented by the monarch, but was limited to levying taxes in the form of fines from those adjudged responsible for the wrong. Execution, maiming, outlawry, or other physical punishments were relatively rare. Order in society, in the sense of what people would tolerate, rested more on the actions of private citizens than on any central political authority.

Anglo-Norman society saw an increasing reliance on physical punishment. Under William certain harms were increasingly seen as having a public quality. If a Norman was killed the Saxon community had to produce the killer or pay a substantial sum (the murdrum fine).

With the Norman appropriation of Saxon land and wealth, it was not surprising that theft was seen no longer merely as an infringement of another's property interests but as a wider threat: in the early twelfth century the hanging of thieves became more frequent. The justification for the inflicting of physical penalties by the courts was the communal interest: these sanctions would not be warranted by the violation of a purely private interest. Despite this, the mobilization of the courts and the gallows was still primarily a matter for the citizen—indeed, the right to erect a gallows was often a franchise granted by the king. The parish constables and 'hue and cry' were adjuncts to a system that relied in the main on individuals' perception of their own interests. While the category of 'crime' developed a more public quality, its enforcement remained private.

But techniques for increased centralized control were of interest to the emergent feudal state on both a political and a social level. In the latter half of the twelfth century Henry II developed a structure of law courts as well as the personnel to run them—keepers of the peace, sheriffs, coroners. Crime and disorder, especially after Stephen's reign, were useful pegs on which to hang the development of institutions which protected and enlarged the sphere of royal interests and influence. Henry II imposed a degree of political stability and central authority after the anarchy of the preceding years, and the evolution of a rudimentary criminal justice system was one means of achieving this.

Rather than with a 'police' force, the initiative for prosecution lay with the presenting jury from the hundred or the county who were under a duty to present the visiting judge with details of all the offences committed since his last visitation. They would be fined if they left any out. This collective responsibility for the village was paralleled by the institution of the office of constable as a rotating one, undertaken in turn by each villager. But the stress on the duty of the community to suppress crime and disorder seems to have lasted only for a short period and the status of the office of constable had declined by Tudor times—the duties were onerous and deputies were paid to undertake them. Crime and punishment remained essentially a private affair throughout medieval and early modern England.

In the heyday of the absolutist and centralized feudal state under the Tudors there was a resurgence of central intervention in the administration of the criminal law. New criminal courts were developed, such as the so-called 'prerogative' courts of which the Star Chamber is the best-remembered; new procedures emerged when the Marian statutes initiated a short-lived attempt by Philip and Mary to turn justices of the peace into quasi-public prosecutors; there were new offences and principles of liability as well as a new reliance on physical forms of punishment. It was a period when more executions appear to have taken place than at any other—Hollinshed alleges that 72,000 thieves were hanged during the reign of Henry VIII.[1] Even allowing for exaggeration, this death toll would be enormous for a country with a total population of some two to three million.

As with the Angevins, the motivation behind the Tudor use of the criminal justice system was threefold: a political struggle by the central authority to strengthen its influence and extend its control over the feudal landholding class; straightforward fiscal advantage; and an underlying objective of strengthening the disciplinary regime for the population as a whole. On a local level, as a means of disciplining the working people, the use of criminal sanctions remained in the hands of the middle and upper classes. How it was used, when and to whom it was applied, were matters for the aggrieved citizen.

This operated well within a status-based feudal society but the transition towards mercantile and industrial capitalism brought changing forms of economic organization and of wealth. In the eighteenth century the criminal justice system evolved to protect these directly, and indirectly brought about changes of attitude towards the idea of 'property' itself. Thompson,[2] in his study of the 1723 Black Act, illustrates how rights over land and game, previously enjoyed by the villagers, were transformed from communal rights to ones which 'belonged' to wealthy individuals. Such a metamorphosis was backed by an unprecedented expansion of penal laws, supported by the death penalty and enforced locally by landholders themselves sitting as JPs. Hay[3] has argued that the judicious mobilization of the majesty of the law through the Assize Courts, through the explicit threat of capital punishment, and through the manipulation of the system (so that the death sentence could be commuted to transportation or imprisonment) protected and extended the social bonds of deference and authority and the property relationships on which these were based. The criminal law provided new skirts for the interests of the proper-tied classes to shelter behind.

In the eighteenth century the patterns of social control and criminal law went together and were mainly centred in civil society rather than in the hands of the State. The Home Office remained embryonic until the nineteenth century and, although it received reports from the country, was in no position to influence day-to-day events. Calling out the army was a last resort, of no long-term value, which only exacerbated anti-government feeling. The older forms of control survived through the feudal land-tie of landlord and tenant or the master–servant relationship in old manufacturing guilds. Regulation of social and economic behaviour was a personal matter, involving the propertied classes in their roles as squires and masters as well as militiamen, magistrates, and sheriffs. In the country the land-tie touched all points of existence—the squire's involvement was not merely with the worker during working hours but encompassed the family, leisure, religion, and politics.

The New Police

This pattern changed dramatically with the emergence of the New Police in 1829. No longer was public safety to be in local, personal, and voluntary hands, characterized by tradition and discretion. Now there was a body of men, hierarchically organized, owing allegiance to senior officers, significantly influenced by central government, and operating according to formal rules of law and procedure. The first of these bodies was created in London by the Metropolitan Police Act in 1829. With the extension of the franchise and democratization of the boroughs, the Municipal Corporations Act in 1835 required 178 boroughs to form Watch Committees for the creation of police forces (not that they all did). The County Police Act 1839 permitted (but did not require) the formation of forces in rural areas as well, a move hastened by the spread of the Chartist movement. Consolidation and compulsion arrived in 1856 when Palmerston steered through the County and Borough Police Act, and by 1857 there were some 239 forces operating in England and Wales.

There were some immediate antecedents for this reform. Before 1829 there had been policing of a sort. The watchmen (4,500 of them in London) were the relics of the old parish constables but they were poorly paid and of low quality. With no organization, there was little they could do to detect or prevent crime. There were some honourable exceptions—in Marylebone the system worked well and in 1843 the parish vestry complained that with the New Police they were worse policed and at a greater cost than they had been in the unreformed days.

Initiatives had been taken on a piecemeal basis: in the 1750s the novelist Henry Fielding and later his blind half-brother Sir John Fielding, acting as magistrates, set up the Bow Street Runners, but this was only a small force financed by the Fieldings themselves. In 1798 another magistrate, Patrick Colquhoun, created the Dock Police and this was put on a statutory footing in 1800. Their purpose was to protect the property of the West Indian sugar merchants from pilfering, although the dockers saw this booty as part of their pay—they would often forgo wages for a 'general licence for plunder' and the development of the police has been portrayed as a method of tying the dockers to wage labour.[4]

The idea of a patrolling force to prevent crime had been taking root in the writings of the Fieldings and Colquhoun during the latter half of the eighteenth century. It fitted well with the utilitarian social philosophy of Bentham and the reformist ideas of Beccaria whose *Essay on Crime and Punishment*, published in 1764, swept across continental Europe and influenced criminal justice reform in many countries. Beccaria preached the need for clear and well-publicized laws, proper procedures at trial, punishment proportional to the offence, the reduction or abolition of the incidence of capital punishment, and reformation as the objective of the prison system. Logically included among these was the requirement of a police force to prevent and detect crime.

These were radical ideas for a century when class authority was a highly personal matter and mobilization of the law or mitigation of the severity of a penalty reinforced that authority. Perhaps it is not surprising that successive parliamentary committees, in 1770, 1793, 1812, 1818, and 1822, failed to produce any effective proposal for policing London. The bills which were put before Parliament were either defeated or quietly dropped. As the 1822 committee put it, 'it is difficult to reconcile an effective police force with that perfect freedom of action and exemption from interference which are the great privileges and blessings of society in this country'.

Opposition to the bills came from the gentry and from the emergent commercial and industrial class. Athough some fears were practical, such as tax increases, both groups opposed the spectre of a state-controlled police on the continental model as a threat to the tradition of local independence. Indeed, they feared any increase in the intervention of the State in the social or the economic world. One factor in Peel's success in pushing the 1829 Act through Parliament was his exemption of the powerful City of London from its provisions, and there is still a separate City of London force, distinct from the Metropolitan police.

By his family background Peel bridged the worlds of landed property and the new commercial classes, and he was personally committed to the establishment of the police force. He set up yet another parliamentary committee in 1828 but ensured that it was dominated by those sharing his views. The Prime Minister, Wellington, supported Peel's reforms: he had observed the continuing failure to suppress public disorder and had not forgotten the demonstrations surrounding Queen Caroline's return from Germany and her funeral. Peel took advantage of Parliament's concentration on the question of Catholic emancipation and steered the 1829 bill through the House with little trouble. Despite the political acumen behind the passing of the legislation, it remains difficult to understand this volte-face by a Parliament which had rejected similar moves only seven years before.

What had become of the sensitivity to 'continental despotism'? In his study of the Act, Lyman[5] has suggested that the continual public disorder and rioting, the hatred surrounding the use of troops, the unpopularity of the monarchy, and the insurgent republican sentiments had increased the demand for protection so much that it crossed party lines. Even so the collapse of the entrenched opposition of constitutionalist libertarians remains surprising. The Reform Bill riots in the early 1830s included calls for the abolition of the New Police, 'Peel's bloody gang'. But the New Police survived the fall of Peel and the election of a Whig administration, although the new government remained equivocal, not to say hostile, towards the Metropolitan police throughout the next decade.

Initial Hostility

The 1829 legislation was skeletal, creating two Commissioners of Police (later reduced to one) who were also Justices of the Peace. Final control was left in the hands of the Home Secretary, who was responsible to Parliament. The detailing of the powers and duties of the police, their organization and structure, were left to Peel and the new Commissioners. Peel paid close attention to his new force until November 1830 when he was replaced by Melbourne. The general instructions issued in 1829 are revealing:

It should be understood at the outset that the object to be attained is the prevention of crime. To this great end every effort of the police is to be directed. The security of person and property and the preservation of a police establishment will thus be better effected than by the detection and punishment of the offender. . . .

He will be civil and obliging to all people of every rank and class. . . .

He must be particularly cautious not to interfere idly or unnecessarily in order to make a display of his authority . . .

The first 'peelers', dressed in top hats, blue swallowtail coats, heavy serge trousers, and boots and equipped with wooden rattles and truncheons, did not look coercive. In September 1829 there were approximately 1,000 constables, and by June 1830 this had swelled to 3,314. They were assailed with names such as 'raw lobsters' and 'blue devils' and were linked in the public's imagination with the anti-reform Tories, the monarchy, and standing armies. When in 1833 a constable was stabbed at a public meeting in Coldbath Fields, the jury at the inquest brought in a verdict of 'justifiable homicide'.

The early London policemen were recruited from those 'who had not the rank, habits or station of gentlemen'. They were often ill-educated countrymen, at least 5 ft. 7 in. tall, strong, and of good character. The only educational standard required was the ability to read and write. Recruiting from outside London prevented both political patronage and partiality towards kith and kin. It also had the effect of insulating the police from the influence of working-class neighbourhoods and allowing them to be less reticent in the use of force.

The developing threat from working-class political movements in the mid-nineteenth century helped to soften the opposition to the police from the middle-class constitutionalists and from the landed gentry. It was the working class that most felt the impact of the reformed police—the 'plague of blue locusts' was met by numbers of anti-police demonstrations, especially between 1839 and 1844. These have been well documented by Storch;[6] for example, in Leeds in June 1844 the appearance of the police at the Green Man beerhouse in York Street touched off massive confrontations that lasted for three days. Storch describes it as a mass uprising against the Leeds Corporation Police, initially led by soldiers but with civilians joining in, according to the local press, not 'out of love to the soldiers themselves, but from . . . feelings of hatred towards the police'.

The opposition to the police was accentuated by the class bias of the criminal law which was readily apparent in areas such as the Game Laws or union legislation, and hostility flared easily: it is significant that a similar pattern of resentment to policing has emerged in the inner cities in the 1980s, again fuelled by discriminatory enforcement of laws such as those against soft drugs and the notorious (and now repealed) 'sus' provisions of the Vagrancy Acts. It was a bitterness felt not only amongst the young but throughout the community.

Throughout the nineteenth century the police were involved in the suppression of union organization and the subversion of industrial action. This bias appeared in the criminal law as well as in the judiciary and the legislature but the decisions of the police to prosecute pickets, disperse demonstrations, or escort non-union labour were not statutory but discretionary. The police were consistently used to neutralize the few weapons held by the working class in industrial conflicts and this use came early in their history—in 1837 Metropolitan policemen were sent to Yorkshire to suppress anti-Poor Law riots. Two years later detachments were despatched all over the country in response to fears about Chartism. Brogden[7] gives examples from Liverpool later in the century:

In the period 1883–94, the Liverpool Head Constable sent detachments to defend the Caernarvonshire quarries against strikers, crossed the city boundary to deal with a seamen's strike in Bootle and the Mersey to terminate a Cheshire saltworkers' strike, into St. Helens to support an employer against his workforce, to Trafalgar Square for a political demonstration and to Lancaster for a racecourse dispute.

Another tactic, the infiltration of working-class organizations, started as early as 1833 when Sergeant William Popay was unmasked as a police spy at a discussion meeting of the National Political Union, having acted as a double agent in the guise of a poor artist for some months. But the 'constitutionalist' opposition to 'government spies' was still strong—a Parliamentary Select Committee censured his conduct and laid down general principles regarding 'plain-clothes' police work. It was not until 1842 that a detective branch was started, though it consisted only of six officers who were seconded from and returned to uniformed duties. But in 1877, after a corruption scandal, the Criminal Investigation Department, of 250 men, was formed under the direction of a lawyer, Howard Vincent. This heralded a new emphasis on undercover work, furthered in 1883 by the creation of the Special Irish Branch of the CID to combat the Fenian bombing campaign. By the First World War the Special Branch had dropped the 'Irish' and its work had spread to cover any 'subversive' political or industrial activity.

But policing in those early days, in pursuance of Peel's objective of preventive policing, consisted mainly of patrolling the streets. Wide-ranging legislation, especially the Metropolitan Police Act, 1839, handed the constable a battery of powers to regulate street behaviour of all kinds, dealing with, among other things, public houses, refreshment houses, unlicensed theatres, gaming houses, prostitutes, obscene books, and games in the streets, and ensuring new standards of orderliness and 'social sanitation'. Preventive policing also involved patrolling working-class districts and clamping down on popular leisure pursuits. Thompson has cogently argued that what could not be regulated by factory employment and the clock was to be cowed by regular deterrent patrols. They 'watched St. Giles to guard St. James'—intruders into middle-class areas were open to arrest under the Vagrancy Laws or s. 64 of the Metropolitan Police Act, 1839. The modern counterpart of this policy is that black youths who venture out of their own areas are liable to be stopped and searched. As one officer put it, 'If I saw a black man walking through Wimbledon High Street, I would definitely stop him. 'Course, down here it's a common sight, so there's no point.'[8] In Victorian England too the beat was a penetration and surveillance of people's everyday actions, not simply at the level of physical control but as a representation of moral and political authority over their lives.

Storch has argued in his study of anti-police riots that the police in Victorian England functioned as a direct complement to the élite urban middle class as they sought to mould the working class to new disciplines in work and in leisure. Legislation, charitable works, and the police were different means of seeking reforms, whether in education, temperance, recreation, or the sabbath: 'Dogfights, cockfights, gambling, popular fetes—always described in contemporary sources as both 'sensual' and 'barbarous'—were symbolic of the fear of social anarchy which always lay beneath the surface of early Victorian professions of optimism.'[9] Establishing moral authority and control over leisure activities away from the workplace was a necessary counterpart to the discipline of the factory itself.

Storch concludes that the police were unsuccessful in their role as 'domestic missionaries' as many of their moralizing campaigns foundered on the impermeability of working-class culture, and his argument is supported by the evidence of enduring anti-police feeling in working-class communities which erupted into small-scale disorders late in the nineteenth century. The failure of attempts to stamp out prostitution, change drinking habits, or limit popular festivals showed the limits of police effectiveness and caused leaders such as Commissioner Mayne to advocate licensing such activities rather than futilely seeking to abolish them through criminal sanctions.

Class and Social Control

Marxist analysts, with their stress on class relations, the role of the State, and the nature of ideology, provide a more satisfying perspective on this history than, say, those who view it as a natural evolution of 'civilization', or liberal theorists who would point to the ideas and ideals of social contract and utilitarian thinkers as the motivating factors behind the change. But at that time there were problems of social control, firmly grounded in the material conditions of life and accentuated by the class divisions arising in the context of the economic and social forces unleashed by the industrialization of Britain.

It was no accident that the impetus to establish police forces should come from the towns where the industrial propertied classes, reluctant to turn out as militiamen, saw it as the government's job to protect them and their property. The old techniques of control that had functioned so well in the homogenous rural communities of eighteenth-century England were no longer adequate to maintain the relative positions of social classes in the new England or to protect the wealth and persons of the propertied classes. This was especially apparent within the towns: London's population doubled in the eighteenth century, from half a million to a million, but then exploded to nearer six million in the nineteenth century. The major shift of population from the country to the towns, largely because of the demands of agricultural capital and the enclosure movement, created an urban proletariat which could sell its labour but had little to fall back on in times of unemployment. In the country the old land-tie had been a more reciprocal arrangement than the urban contracts of employment—deference and charity had gone hand in hand.

In the early decades of the nineteenth century, the deepening of the class divide and of social and economic inequality, accentuated by the ending of the Napoleonic Wars, caused the urban poor to suffer acute unemployment and unprecedented poverty. The growth of a large surplus population had its utility for industrial capital with its need for a large and flexible pool of labour and the consequent depression of wages. But there were inherent problems—such a population would scarcely remain docile without the squire or the reverend to keep moral order. Nor could the capitalist employer of wage labour present himself in the same light of social authority as the landholder. Class conflict was much nearer the surface of everyday life. The warnings—the increasing number of property offences and the capacity of the working class to organize politically—could no longer be ignored. The Luddites and Captain Swing, Peterloo and later the Chartists, were all clear signals of the danger to that 'social harmony' of the market place necessary for the new mode of production and capitalist accumulation.

The machinery of state in the nineteenth century also saw changes—the response to such threats had to come from a significant initiative by the State rather than from powerful individuals. The factory posed the employer–worker conflict in sharper relief than the old feudal land-holding relationships: if the government was to intervene, it would have to be in a manner that appeared independent and neutral. Such intervention was not merely in the area of crime and the police but across a range of education and welfare issues that had previously been matters for private individuals. Only in this way could the deep-seated class conflicts be concealed and the working class transformed into a docile workforce. This was the process of incorporation into the framework of the liberal-democratic State and of consent to the parliamentary road and the rule of law. As Peel himself put it, 'The enforcement of the law compromises no opinion on political questions and it enables the Government to speak with a tone of authority, not only to the party against whose acts the law may be immediately directed, but to other parties, who may be carried beyond due bounds in their preparations for resistance or self-defence. It deprives them of the pretext that the law does not afford protection or redress.'

The emergence of the police was not merely a reaction to the problems of urban order in the face of the industrial revolution, but also involved the central problem of the legitimacy of the State itself. The removal of the State and the law from close identification with the capitalist class was a necessary step for the establishment of capitalist hegemony. Bunyan[10] has referred to this battle as one of 'ideological attrition', with the police as part of a strategy aiming to co-opt the working class into co-operation with a particular form of state which was necessary to preserve and develop capitalism as the dominant economic mode of production.

The Creation of Consent

Imposition of repressive control will never be successful—as noted above, there was an early hostility to and rejection of the 'New Police'. But this was gradually replaced by a slowly manufactured co-operation between police and people: 'In each neighbourhood, and sometimes street by street, the police negotiated a complex, shifting, largely unspoken "contract".'[11] Ignatieff describes this as the 'microscopic basis of police legitimacy'. It was an acceptance that had real conditions attached—if the police stepped over the boundaries, co-operation would be withdrawn and suspicion renewed until the whole fragile edifice had been re-erected.

The nineteenth-century policeman very quickly became a constitutional symbol (though with this undercurrent of ambivalence) of the legitimacy of the State—the middle classes soon became reconciled to the principle, especially since the structure of the new forces also meant that control was vested firmly in their hands. That this also held true for the workers was shown when proposals to expand police powers to counter the 'garrotting' panic of the 1860s were greeted by the socialist *Reynolds* newspaper as 'converting the English Peeler into a species of continental policeman . . . the mouchard or spy'. Such constitutional concern is reminiscent of the anxieties of the gentry a century earlier. The dreaded 'Peeler' (originally a pejorative term but now affectionate) had become the personification of the liberties of the true-born Englishman.

The police had become the embodiment of the 'rule of law' rather than of an executive power wielded by the government. They were seen as independent from the State, accountable for their actions, neutral, using minimum force, and providing services to the whole community, both in the effective prevention of crime and in a broader helping role. For the Marxist these characteristics are essentially ideological, concealing the true nature of the class interests underlying them. Yet these features are not mere smokescreens. They have real substance and value—the British police always have used significantly less violence than their counterparts abroad. The paradox does not undermine the usefulness of seeing the police in ideological terms. Thompson[12] expresses it fluently when he discusses the ideological nature of the 'rule of law':

Moreover, people are not as stupid as some structuralist philosophers suppose them to be. They will not be mystified by the first man who puts on a wig. It is inherent in the especial character of the law, as a body of rules and procedures, that it shall apply logical criteria with reference to standards of universality and equality. . . . If the law is evidently partial and unjust, then it will mask nothing, legitimise nothing, contribute nothing to any class's hegemony. . . . The law may be rhetoric, but it need not be empty rhetoric.

Mutatis mutandis, this applies effectively in the context of the police—the constitutional constraints may well be analysed in ideological terms but they may (quite consistently) be valued for what they are.

The first of these characteristics, vital in ensuring consent, was separation from the State—a nationally organized police under a separate ministry would have placed the police constitutionally as part of the executive, identifiable with the government of the day. In a society without a written constitution delineating the rights of the individual *vis-à-vis* the State, opponents of such proposals feared that too much power would be placed in the hands of the executive. Of course, the 1829 Act linked the Home Office and the Metropolitan Police Commissioners, but the tradition of local government was a different affair in the provinces—London has remained unique and the relationship between the Home Secretary and the Commissioner is still ambiguous and ill-defined. The first Commissioners—Charles

Rowan, a soldier, and Richard Mayne, a barrister—established a considerable degree of operational autonomy. This had its limits: in 1887 the Commissioner, Warren, was forced by the Home Secretary to resign. This was partly due to the militaristic and violent policing of socialist demonstrations in Trafalgar Square, but Warren was also unwilling to submit to the Home Secretary's authority.

There was no lack of political will on the part of the government to concentrate the control of the police in their own hands, and a Select Committee in 1853 received evidence that the various police forces knew little of what the others were doing and co-operated less. One witness was Edwin Chadwick, a social reformer whose writings had played an important part in the creation of the Metropolitan Police, who had been a member of the 1836 Royal Commission on the Constabulary, and who now was arguing for an efficient national police. Following this, two abortive bills engineered by Palmerston envisaged a greater degree of central control over the provincial forces. But that battle had already been lost with the Municipal Corporations Act, 1835 which required the reformed boroughs to set up Watch Committees to oversee the policing arrangements. Interfering with that independence proved politically and physically dangerous—angry delegations of mayors met in London in 1854, passed resolutions condemning the proposals of the 1853 committee, and forced themselves into Palmerston's office; there was much sneering at the 'spies' in the new proposals for an inspectorate of constabulary, and traditional local government independence was proclaimed to be under threat.

Although the 1856 County and Borough Police Act opted for the small decentralized force, this did not lead to control by democratic means. Control in the boroughs involved the members of local élites who formed the Watch Committees and exerted considerable influence over policing objectives: 'the Chairman of the Watch Committee was the attorney for large liquor interests in the town while another member was the physician for most of the brothels. Needless to say, the activities of the police, in respect to liquor and prostitution, were negligible.'[13] David Phillips[14] has highlighted the collaboration between the police, the coalmasters, and the magistracy in enforcing low wages in the Black Country in the 1850s, and, as Glover[15] puts it, 'public confidence was no doubt largely engendered by the confidence placed in the New Police by the shop-keepers'. Retailers exhorted the police to act against hawkers, the clergy urged curbs on Sunday recreational activities, and factory owners used the police to prevent 'thefts' from the workplace. The middle classes were rapidly won over—by the time of the 1926 General Strike the readers of *The Times* alone contributed £250,000 to police charities.

It has been argued that the chief officers of police forces gained an early autonomy from sectional interests, particularly in the counties where the authority was based on the magistracy, itself dominated by the gentry. But the archetypal small decentralized force was bound to reflect the immediate interests of the politically powerful—a link that was only to be broken after the First World War with the emergence of Labour-controlled local authorities.

The 1856 legislation ensured that all towns and counties would have police forces but the only centralizing measure was the provision of an Inspectorate of Constabulary based at and reporting to the Home Office. Even this had to be paid for—the Treasury met 25 per cent of the cost of efficient forces. Despite the expense, it gave the inspectors a considerable financial lever to ensure that proper standards were maintained. Initially there were two inspectors; a third was added in 1857. Today there are five. Many of the county forces and those in the larger boroughs passed the first inspection. But in the smaller boroughs, Critchley[16] describes some of the arrangements as 'farcical'—in Totnes, Devon, there were two elderly sergeants-at-mace, aged 65 and 74, and in Sandwich, Kent, the single constable was also the town hairdresser.

Increasing acceptance was reinforced by an awareness that the force was not merely acting in an arbitrary and unregulated fashion but was accountable. This did not mean that there was popular control of the police—the Watch Committees were dominated by landed and business élites. But in the early years there was close and detailed judicial supervision of police action: had the power of arrest been properly exercised?, should the suspect have been interrogated?, should evidence obtained by improper means be admitted? After the 1850s justices of the peace increasingly abandoned any inquisitorial role and left investigation and interrogation to the police. They also developed the reliance on police evidence that characterizes modern courts: the independent regulation of the police still demonstrated publicly that they too were bound by legal rules and procedures, both inside and outside the courtroom. In these early years there was also parliamentary scrutiny—in 1833 the police were both castigated at the Popay inquiry and reprimanded by a Select Committee for using unnecessary violence in breaking up a demonstration at Coldbath Fields.

The public were also reassured by the severe discipline to which police constables were subjected. They could be fined, reduced in rank, or summarily dismissed: in the first thirty years of the Metropolitan force nearly one-third were dismissed and similar proportions were recorded in the provincial forces (most of the dismissals were for drunkenness). A high number of officers resigned 'voluntarily' but without pension or gratuity (although many went to join other forces). The sight of constables themselves subjected to a harsh authority must have contributed to their acceptance by the public as 'only doing their job'.

At the street level, despite their class allegiance, the police operated on an impartial basis—the Metropolitan force recruited from outside London for this very reason. Within the family or in the community, though not necessarily at the workplace, there was no partisan dealing out of justice. Their impartiality was encouraged, after their slow disengagement from the self-interested tentacles of the Watch Committees, by the neutrality embedded in the bureaucratic procedures that differed so markedly from the personal enforcement of the law in earlier eras.

A statutory ban on political involvement, reinforcing their institutional neutrality, left policemen disenfranchised until 1887. But there were attempts at union orgainization and at affiliation with the labour movement. This was always likely to be difficult because of the basic paradox: a policeman is working-class in that he is dependent on the sale of his labour and has no power over the labour of others, but politically he plays a significant part in ensuring the domination of capital over labour. The police themselves were always prevented from forging links with organized labour, from attempting to form a representative body, or even from having the right to confer. Bitterness over pay, rest days, and pensions swelled up in the ranks of London policemen in 1872 and 1890 but this was immediately stamped upon by the Metropolitan Commissioner—100 strikers were sacked in 1872, although they were reinstated after expressing 'contrition' to senior officers. The thirty-nine who were sacked in 1890 did not get a second chance.

The last opportunity for the police to identify with organized labour was during the First World War. Police pay had again failed to keep up with the cost of living and the clandestine National Union of Police and Prison Officers was formed. On 30 August 1918 a major national police strike including 6,000 London policemen, caused Lloyd George to speak of the possibility of revolution. He met NUPPO leaders and agreed to meet their conditions, and a Representative Board dominated by the union was set up. At the same time, Sir Edward Henry was sacked and Sir Nevil Macready, from the Tonypandy riots, was made Metropolitan Commissioner in his place. Improvements in pay and conditions bought off demands for recognition of the union itself. The Desborough Committee in 1919 advocated major pay rises but also recommended that a non-union Police Federation be set up, that there be a ban on a police union, and that it be made a criminal offence to induce a policeman to strike. This passed into the Police Act, 1919 which also debarred policemen from joining or affiliating with outside trade unions. NUPPO's last stand, an attempt to bring about a nationwide strike behind the union, was a fiasco—only Liverpool turned out in numbers, and they found themselves facing troops with fixed bayonets and tanks. The leaders of NUPPO were all sacked and the union threat diminished, not to resurface until the 1970s when again, after threatening to campaign for the right to strike, the police found themselves the beneficiaries of large pay rises. The Police Federation, though originally an active pressure group, had its efficacy reduced by being divided into three sections, constables, sergeants, and inspectors, preventing undue influence from the more radical constables.

If we turn from the organization of the force to its tactics, it is clear that from the earliest days most forces relied on the strategy of minimum force—the use of firearms or sabres was rare, although cutlasses were originally issued for night patrolling. Truncheons were seen as a defensive weapon and were concealed until 1863, just as guns are in the 1980s. Even when policing strikes or demonstrations the police relied on creating a felt presence rather than on dispersing crowds through physical force. This does not mean to say, as Geary[17] has shown, that there are no examples of police brutality, witness Tom Mann's account of the seamen's strike in Liverpool in 1911:

If the worst and most ferocious brutes in the world had been on the scene, they would not have displayed such brutality as the Liverpool City Police, and their imported men ... such a scene of brutal butchery was never witnessed in Liverpool before. Defenceless men and women, several of whom were knocked down by heavy blows from the truncheons of powerful men, and even as the crowd fled from the onslaught, the police still continued to batter away at them ...[18]

Such cases were exceptional. But minimum force did not mean no force. It simply implied that an officer must face a real and immediate threat before using violence.

Visible patrolling also meant that people could see at first hand the contribution constables made to the community. They were inevitably a resource to be called on to resolve conflicts or to provide services. One effect of the new police was on crime rates—from the 1850s to the First World War there was a clear decline in recorded crime. For example, from 1857 to 1911 the incidence of assaults decreased from 67.5 to 24.1 per 100,000. Since the development of a police force would be an incentive to report, investigate, and prosecute crime, one would expect more crime to be recorded—the statistical decline suggests that there was actually a fall in the crime rate and that the real rate of decline was steeper than that marked by the official figures. How much of this is attributable to the reform of the police is debatable—just as the increase in 'crime' during the first decades of the nineteenth century has been explained by the social and economic dislocation of the transition to an industrial society, so the decline could be put down to the increasing stability and relative prosperity in the latter part of the century. But the police serviced communities in other ways, whether by providing information or assistance for people in difficulty or by offering an external referee to be appealed to in quarrels within families or between neighbours. One of those services must undoubtedly have been providing access to the courts through help and advice with prosecutions. By the 1880s the London police were playing a large part not just in the investigation and detection of crime but also in the prosecution of offences.

This history seeks to explore the police as a particular technique of social control, emerging at a time when the dominance of industrial capital gave a distinct and sharp quality to class conflict. Control had, above all, to be exercised by a neutral agency in order to be accepted as legitimate and to be at all effective. The need for such a force was irresistible, yet it clashed with a rejection (shared by the agrarian rich and the new industrial entrepreneurs) of expanded central executive power. These constitutionalist arguments had their roots in the traditional local quality of English government as well as in the parliamentary struggles against the king in the seventeenth century. The battle was as much about the limits of legitimate state intervention as about the police. This battle was responsible for the form of the new police—small forces under local control.

But the consent of the population was also essential and was gradually won when the police were seen to act on certain principles (independence, accountability, neutrality), unarmed, and as providers of real services to the community.

This language of consent is echoed in the 1980s in the ideas of community policing or neighbourhood watch. As in the mid-nineteenth century the language has important ideological connotations but also expresses values (the central elements of police legitimacy) which it is important to maintain. The central thesis of this book is that, although the liberal and constitutionalist characteristics of the police mask their true relationship with the state, they are not mere hypocrisy. The task is to put substance into the rhetoric.

3

The 'New' Police

Traditional Limits

Dixon has been replaced by Darth Vader as the image of the British bobby, at least according to Reiner. The friendly, approachable constable, dealing with people as people and responding to their problems, has given way to an anonymous and alien figure, backed by the resources of high technology and overwhelming force. This image reflects the subtle but inexorable change that has taken place in the relationship between the police and the public. The constant appeal from both urban and rural communities to see more constables on the beat reflects the decline of policing as a service industry. The word 'service' connotes that policing is about responding to demands, within the limits of legal powers. It does not imply the creation and instigation of policies generated within the police themselves. In a service role, police intervention is kept at a minimal level, whether they are dealing with complaints of crime, containing public disorder, or handling disputes. Within this context, the Peel maxim 'prevention of crime' is interpreted narrowly.

The service role of the police has been a product of constraints on power, originally imposed in the nineteenth century and specifying that governments should not be closely identified with particular policing policies, that there are legal boundaries to police powers, that there is a local organizational structure with an absence of centralized control, and that there are restraints on the economic and technical resources available to the police. All these are features of a society based on constitutional consensus and are conspicuous by their absence in totalitarian or colonial situations where consent to policing is not sought and the objective of policing is the coercion of the population in the interests of a dominant class or élite.

In an authoritarian regime, some or all of these elements of constitutional policing may be absent—there will almost certainly be a close identification between government policy and police actions; there are likely to be wide and arbitrary powers; substantial resources will be made available; few limits on the use of force will be observed. The police are unlikely to be held to account for actions, expenditure, or policy, either in a democratic or in a legal forum, except to an executive which itself dictates operational policy.

Fascist and colonial societies are always constitutionally unstable in the medium term. In a liberal democracy the symbolic neutrality of the police aids trust in (and thus the stability of) political institutions and that symbolism is of particular importance in Britain, which has no formal Bill of Rights or constitution. Written constitutions directly express the relationship of the individual to the collective, the rights and duties of both citizen and state, but in Britain we lack any fundamental and explicit expression of these. So when the State impinges on the life of an individual we often dramatize the encounter and thereby symbolize cardinal features of the constitutional relationship.

The office of the constable in particular and the criminal justice system as a whole is a peculiarly sensitive indicator, as it is there that the State has the legal power to take physical control of the body of the subject, the ultimate assertion of power and authority. The exercise of such power is inevitably closely scrutinized and where the police abuse their authority—as with the Special Branch raid on the BBC in Glasgow in January 1987 which seized film and documents on the *Secret Society* series—there are immediate calls to provide constitutional safeguards through a Bill of Rights. But for most of the time the criminal justice system is a touchstone by which the English judge themselves and their society: in echoing the tourist's cry, 'Your policemen are wonderful!', they congratulate themselves on the stability and superiority of Anglo-Saxon social organization.

The symbol of the police constable, still very evocative of the central values of liberal society, has begun to dissolve over the past twenty-five years as certain key characteristics of the traditional service function of policing have been transformed—notably the weakening of local influence over the police and the consequent strengthening of police autonomy and national political control; the replacement of the traditional foot patrol by car patrols on the one hand and special squads on the other; the re-equipping of the force with a modern arsenal and riot-control equipment, and the willingness to deploy them. The resources available for policing (personnel, material, and legal) have increased and there has been a deeper level of surveillance of the population through security agencies and greater intervention in the home and the family.

Increasing intervention is a key feature of the changing police force—the involvement of the constable in the school, the home, or the workplace is not posited on the actual or threatened commission of offences but on a broader conception of 'troublemakers' and those who might become 'police customers' in the future. The rationale rests on a broad understanding of the police remit of preventing crime—a widely conceived social intervention will have its impact on future crime figures. There is a parallel in the expansion of the undercover activities of Special Branch, who keep watch on potential 'subversion' not only when illegal means are likely to be employed but also when the political and industrial action envisaged is lawful.

The higher political profile of the Police Federation and the Association of Chief Police Officers mirrors this increased involvement, with their public pronouncements constantly stressing moral values and suggesting simplistic explanations not merely of crime but of all forms of social disruption. With the declining influence of the Church as arbiter of the moral order, the police often seem to take on the status of secular priests or social psychologists. 'Newman lists society's ills' was the headline of a *Guardian* article in 1985, reporting a speech by the Metropolitan Police Commissioner in which he blamed television, easy credit, drugs, unemployment, and left-wing politicians for the rise in crime. When they issue edicts such as these and are taken seriously, the police are no longer acting just as protectors of the community but are actively participating in the construction and reconstruction of the moral order.

The Organization of Forces

A useful starting-point for examining these changes is the 1964 Police Act, based on the 1962 Report of the Royal Commission on the Police. The Commission was set up in 1959 as a result of general concern about rising crime rates in the post-war years, unrest about pay and conditions within the force, and especially after several well-publicized contretemps between Chief Constables and their Watch

Committees which had brought the constitutional relationship between the two into sharp focus.

The Police Act (and the Local Government Act 1972) finally broke with the ideal of a small, local, decentralized force accountable to the community. In 1857 there had been some 239 such forces, many with just a handful of officers policing small towns. A century later there were still 117 separate forces in England and Wales. Subsequent amalgamations have now reduced this to forty-three—forty-one provincial forces and two London forces, the Metropolitan and the City of London. The provincial forces may retain a link with a particular county (Kent), a conurbation (West Midlands), or a loosely defined region (Thames Valley), but the relationship between a force and a specific community has effectively been broken.

The control of the police involves an ill-defined triangular relationship between the chief officers, the local authority, and the Home Office—this will be explored in detail in Chapter 8. Everyday command is in the hands of the Chief Constables (in London known as Commissioners) whose duties under s. 5 of the Police Act are the direction and control of their forces. The Chief Constable is an independent office holder under the Crown and as such is not responsible to any government minister or department, except for the Metropolitan and City of London Commissioners who answer to the Home Secretary.

However, the Chief Constables are bound by statute to report to a Local Police Authority (LPA), successors in title to the old Watch Committees. Their duties, as defined by s. 4 of the Police Act, are to ensure that the force is adequate and efficient. LPAs consist of a combination of local magistrates and councillors, either from the shire or from the metropolitan district. In London the situation is slightly different—the Home Secretary takes the role of police authority. This is derived from the original Metropolitan Police Act, 1829 according to which the Commissioners shall perform such duties as 'shall be from time to time directed by one of his Majesty's principal secretaries of state'. Neither London ratepayers nor their councils have any direct constitutional means of making their views on policing known, although there are now consultative committees set up under the Police and Criminal Evidence Act 1984, the organization of which is the responsibility of the Metropolitan Police Commissioner. Despite this reform, many London boroughs (as well as other cities such as Sheffield and Manchester) have set up their own independent police committees.

The interpretation placed on their respective statutory duties meant that after 1964 LPAs generally regarded themselves as quartermasters, overseeing the budget, receiving an annual report, but not taking initiatives in the policing of an area. In practice such an approach increased the Chief Constable's autonomy so that issues of operational policy came to be seen as outside the competence of the police authority. This 'separation of powers' has been increasingly challenged over the past ten years, particularly in conurbations with a Labour majority on the police authority, as in Liverpool and Manchester, although no significant control has yet been exerted over the activities of Chief Constables. On the financial front they have been outflanked by direct Home Office funding, for instance for the mass policing of NUM picket lines throughout 1984–5. Chief Constables, particularly James Anderton in Greater Manchester, have consistently refused to explain or justify particular operations or account for specific policies. The limited role of the police authority was further weakened by a divisional court ruling in December 1986 that the Home Secretary did not have to gain the consent of the authority before supplying the Northumbria force with plastic bullets—the Home Secretary was exercising a royal prerogative in supplying the equipment and this was not blocked by any law. The decision whether to use it was for the Chief Constable alone to make.

But while the police have largely shaken themselves free from local democratic control, they have achieved no independence from national government. There is substantial Home Office involvement in the appointment of Chief Constables because, although this is formally in the hands of the local police authority, they are required to work from a short-list approved by the Home Office. There are similar restrictions on the authority's power to dismiss its chief officers, a power which again needs Home Office approval.

The Home Office also frequently issues 'advisory' circulars to all forces, making recommendations on all aspects of policing. (It is a brave Chief Constable who treats them as merely 'advisory'.) Their dissemination depends on the Inspectorate of Constabulary, set up in 1856, which is based on, and reports to, the Home Office. Initially the Inspectorate played a major role in deciding whether a force was efficient enough to qualify for central government funding, now

50 per cent of police budgets. Although there is little cause to withhold, or threaten to withhold, central funding for failure to meet required standards, considerable attention to detail is involved in inspections and forces attach great importance to criticisms. In 1983 Circular 114/83 on manpower, efficiency, and economy ordained that the financial constraints and cost effectiveness that had been the watchword in other public sectors would also apply to the police service. The efficacy of forces in carrying out these reforms will be monitored by the Inspectorate.

Furthermore, the Inspectors act as conveners of regional and national meetings of Chief Constables, which in themselves encourage a considerable standardization of policy and approach. This consensus is strengthened by the increasing involvement of the Association of Chief Police Officers (ACPO), one of whose initiatives has been to draw up a joint tactical and operational manual (although this has never been published).

The triangular relationship established by the 1964 Police Act between the Chief Constables, the Home Office, and the local police authorities was intended to construct a system of checks and balances on the powers of each party, preventing any single body from obtaining monopoly control over the police. But the balance has shifted away from the local and towards a national force, with the emphasis on the Chief Constable/Home Office axis. The ease with which the police can be mobilized as a national force was demonstrated during the NUM–NCB dispute in 1984–5. The Association of Chief Police Officers (ACPO) had previously organized the National Reporting Centre to deal with the logistics of the provision of mutual aid between forces under s. 14(3) of the Police Act. This provision enables Chief Constables to furnish other forces with personnel and material, a practice which was originally codified in the Police Act, 1890 but goes back to the earliest years of the police when, for example, Metropolitan officers were sent all over the country to assist in anti-Poor Law riots, strikes, and criminal investigation.

But the National Reporting Centre as a system of co-ordinating requests for help from hard-pressed forces only came into existence after 1972. Since then it has been activated on occasions such as the prison officers' dispute of 1980–1, the inner-city disturbances in 1981, and the papal visit in 1982. It was created on the initiative of ACPO, without local authority or parliamentary debate, though inevitably with Home Office consent. ACPO presents it in straight-forward terms as providing increased efficiency in management, but there is some evidence that the Centre has provided national executive command of the police, initiating and overseeing policies and not merely acting as a conduit for improved communications and movement of personnel. The miners' strike was the Centre's most important test. One example of their effectiveness came in September 1984 when there was a co-ordinated initiative by the government and the National Coal Board to encourage strikers to return to work. Throughout the country 'working' miners were collected from their homes and driven to work in police convoys through picket lines that were suddenly hemmed in by officers from many other forces. The national scale of this operation illustrated the Centre's capacity to co-ordinate police activities, as well as co-operating with the National Coal Board and government. The presence of a Home Office representative at Scotland Yard, the NRC's headquarters, throughout the dispute showed how easily that body might be put under political control.

In organizational terms, the past twenty years have seen a swing to fewer and larger forces, under the close control of the Chief Constable, backed by a Home Office with significant influence. Local independence is now a shadow of its former self, although it had always been a major characteristic of the English state, one which prevented a governing party from forming too close an identification with policing policies or from using the force as a private army. Of course, in a broader sense, there never has been any such animal as a police force reflecting an ideal balance of the 'local' and the 'independent'. The police inevitably reflect and reinforce the structure of social and economic authority embodied in law, in government, and in conventional morality. To hark back to a golden age of local autonomy would be Utopian nostalgia.

The arguments made in 1962 by the Royal Commission in favour of a local/regional structure rather than a national organization with a minister with parliamentary responsibility may have been overtaken by events but they have not been invalidated. In the absence of a written constitution guaranteeing fundamental rights, the independence of the police from central government is a demonstration that the rule of law should not be manipulated by the ruling party. But while a measure of independence for Chief Constables still exists, this has become distorted by the decline in local involvement. The real axis of power has swung from Chief Constable/LPA to Chief Constable/Home Office.

The Specialists

Fundamental change has also taken place at the sharp end of policing—contact with the population. The traditional image was that of the patrolling officer. Peel dressed his officers in blue serge and a top hat and left them unarmed precisely to show that constables were not the military and embodied not the threat of physical force but the law. They could only mobilize the law, by arrest and prosecution, to the same extent that any other citizen might. Acting by themselves, constables were also limited in other ways—you can inflict only so much harm with a truncheon; pursuit on foot is slow; you need to use substantial measures of conciliation and avoid coercion. The image of the unarmed patrolman, knowing the patch and the people, dealing with their problems and yet ready to take on the unexpected, was slowly elevated into the myth that this was the front-line and core of policing. It may not represent the reality of the modern police career but until after the Second World War it approximated to the everyday world of most constables.

For any occupation we tend to create an ideal image of the worker at grassroots—the teacher at the blackboard, the nurse at the bedside, the social worker in the home. In all these cases, as with the constable, career structures actually create pressure to get away from this level as soon as possible—it carries little status and limited rewards. It is almost impossible to get promotion and still continue the same work. There is no career future for the constable who wishes to remain on the beat or in community policing. To advance, the officer needs to transfer to some specialist grouping, in particular CID, Traffic, or Headquarters, and to achieve this ambitious constables must make themselves conspicuous with arrests and prosecutions to their credit. There are no rewards for inactivity, regardless of the orderliness of the beat. Yet the success of community policing requires the long-term assignment of officers to specific beats.

The gap between the ideal of the beat and the reality of a police career has been widening since the 1960s. Unit Beat Policing was introduced as a grand scheme to reorganize patrolling with personal radios, Panda cars for emergency cover, and area officers for continuity. Alderson[1] has argued that this brought about unforeseen and radical changes in the function of the police and in their relations with the public. The advent of patrol cars made the links with the population more tenuous as the officer in the car became difficult to identify and even harder to pass the time of day with. Reaction to the police must also have been affected—there is an aggression in flashing blue lights and sirens which provokes a hostility not aroused by a constable on an old-fashioned bicycle. In the 1980s the impact of ideas on community policing and the demands of community liaison groups have led to many forces reinstating or increasing the number of foot patrols.

But it is the beat that will always be undermanned, not Headquarters, Traffic, or CID. Officers are withdrawn from patrolling to fill gaps elsewhere, whether in manning the station, public order work, or, as we shall see, working in specialist squads. The beat will still be trodden by the younger and less experienced constables or those whose careers have not been successful in conventional police terms: although there may be officers whose ambitions are centred on good beat work, there will be many others who may be termed 'uniform carriers', routinely doing the minimum and working towards their pension.

The derogation from the traditional bobby's role has been accentuated by the increasing number of specialist squads, operating on criteria different from those traditionally employed in police work. The earliest was the Special Irish Branch, established to deal with the Fenian campaigns in the 1880s; now there are separate squads for drugs, robberies, fraud, obscene publications, terrorists, firearms, public order, and so on. There is an obvious managerial justification for having a group concentrate on a particular issue, with special skills and detailed knowledge both of the area and of the relevant legislation. Unco-ordinated and desultory attempts within and across forces to combat the large-scale importation of heroin or to investigate connected killings would rightly provoke public indignation.

Although most large organizations would recognize the logic of this approach, within the police it raises several problems. Primarily it reduces the status of the 'general practitioner' constables to that of conduit pipes, passing on all important matters to someone else. The specialist squads treat themselves as the élites and local officers as lesser brethren. Ordinary divisional officers often find their efforts overwhelmed, as happened in April 1979 at Southall when negotiations between community leaders and police community liaison officers were ignored in the policing of the National Front election meeting.

Over thirty forces have developed 'public-order' squads. Until 1987 the most notorious of these was the Metropolitan's Special Patrol Group, though other forces know it by names such as Tactical Aid Group, Tactical Patrol Group, or Task Force. Manwaring-White[2] draws the parallel between these units and army platoons. The Metropolitan Squad was set up in 1965 to be a mobile support unit that could be quickly moved to the scene of any disturbance. By 1986 there were six units with 280 officers, all specially trained and equipped with weaponry and riot-control equipment available in unmarked Transit vans. They are held on permanent standby, unlike the ordinary support units which, although trained in riot-control techniques, are normally engaged in routine divisional duties.

The Scarman Report is a detailed account of SPG operations in Lambeth, especially in April 1981. It reveals how the 'hard' policing employed showed little local knowledge or sensitivity to issues in a multi-racial community. Progress, such as it was, in police–community relations had been reduced to a shambles. Indeed, neither community leaders nor home beat officers were notified of the operation against street crime, SWAMP '81. The saturation policing utilized arbitrary roadblocks, the stopping and searching of pedestrians, and mass detention—943 stops, 118 arrests, and 75 charges were made, only one of which was for robbery. Scarman's conclusions were that the operation was a 'serious mistake', not consistent with sound principles of policing, and that senior command in 'L' District had not been sufficiently adjusted to the problems of policing a multi-racial community.

The aggressive and confrontational approach of such squads has brought continuous criticism—after the Red Lion Square demonstration in 1974 where Kevin Gately was killed; after the policing of the pickets at Grunwicks in 1977; and after the death of Blair Peach in the wake of a National Front election meeting in Southall in 1979. Eventually, following an internal inquiry, the SPG was disbanded in 1987 to be replaced by eight Territorial Support Groups based on the area commands. However, each of the new units is still based on a nucleus of SPG officers. Each unit will consist of ninety-six constables, seventeen of whom are trained in firearms. They will serve for a four-year period and will support uniform patrolling and plain-clothes surveillance, but they will also have to act in the traditional SPG role in dealing with incidents of terrorism or public disorder.

Organizing policing in this manner, making it more authoritarian and coercive, changes the nature of the relationship with the public. As Scarman pointed out, such exercises have little effect on crime figures. They are more significant as demonstrations of the military muscle that the police can bring to bear on communities which they view as troublesome.

The dangers inherent in specialist public-order squads maintained on a permanent footing have been regularly demonstrated, not least in the exacerbation of violence that they cause when nominally seeking to control crowds. Simply because they are permanent, they are employed in cases previously dealt with by divisional officers. There is a further danger in the weaponry which SPG units carry, enhancing the likelihood that guns will be used unnecessarily. In 1973 two Pakistani youths took hostages in India House. They were armed only with imitation firearms and a knife but were shot and killed by officers of the SPG, again illustrating that defensive, minimum force is adhered to more in word than in action.

In February 1987, a Home Office report suggested that all forces should maintain a specialist firearms unit. Many already do, although they are rarely seen in public. In London, where they are known as the Tactical Firearms Unit, D11, or the Blue Berets, their debut was at the Balcombe Street siege in 1975 when four members of the Provisional IRA held a middle-aged couple hostage for six days before surrendering. Ten years later, after the shooting of WPC Fletcher, they surrounded the Libyan Peoples' Bureau. At their base at Lippits Hill in Essex they are responsible for general firearms training. As a squad they have not been responsible for any injuries or deaths by shooting.

Is there any need for such specialists? In terms of ordinary crime they will have little effect—the average armed robbery lasts a very short time. A sniper might be of use when a siege has developed and hostages are in immediate danger. But why should there be police units where army equivalents already exist? The timescale allows the mobilization of an army unit just as easily as that of a police squad. Where there are army skills as yet undeveloped by the police the military have been called in. With the Iranian Embassy siege in 1980 there was a pressing need for drastic action when a hostage was killed. The commando skills of the SAS Special Operations Group were deployed to bring the siege to an end.

Are the sharpshooting and commando skills of the army to be used in preference to developing permanent police squads? The bloody end of the Iranian Embassy siege (only one of the hostage-takers survived to stand trial) suggests that the police are right to resist military intervention in peacetime—soldiers shoot first, and even under police command the threshold of violence would probably be lowered even further. Close identification with the army would also endanger the image of neutrality. But while any army involvement in everyday life should be closely examined and resisted, does this justify creating police squads for each of forty-three separate forces?

Objections such as these have less validity when the police are dealing with substantial and serious offences such as organized fraud or robbery. In the early 1970s the Metropolitan's Robbery Squad succeeded in combatting a rise in bank robberies, especially through the use of 'supergrass' evidence. Similarly, targeting offences and offenders led to the break-up of East End gangs led by Charles Richardson and the Krays in the 1960s. In the 1980s Scotland Yard's criminal intelligence squad, C11 (specializing in secret surveillance), and the Robbery Squad have slowly cleared up the £26 m Brinks Matt bullion robbery at Heathrow in November 1983.

There is considerable agreement about the importance of this work, often viewed as the core of the police job. But the 'war' attitudes employed can spill over into more controversial areas where the overall impact on the community is greater. The enforcement of the Misuse of Drugs Act gives the police the power to stop and search on the basis of 'reasonable suspicion', yet the Policy Studies Institute Report on the Metropolitan Police stated that only one in twelve of such stops led to further action. The activities of drugs squads have been seen as intrusive and have created hostility within a neighbourhood.

While some specialist work is essential, the main criticism of such squads is that, success being measured by arrests and convictions, the means come to seem less important than the ends and techniques often border on the unacceptable—the use of *agents provocateurs*, undercover officers, supergrasses, violations of the rules over the surveillance and searching of premises and the seizure of evidence, over-enthusiastic interrogation of suspects, or unjustified detention.

Moreover, specialist squads breed a symbiotic relationship between the police and those engaged in criminal activities. Cox, Shirley, and Short[3] have shown how drugs-squad officers in the 1970s allowed certain dealers to operate unhindered in order to obtain information on the rest of the illegal drugs market. In return for providing some of their customers as 'bodies' for the police, they would be paid, not in money, but in 're-cycled' drugs seized by the police in previous raids.

Sometimes such close relationships can lead to outright corruption—the head of the Metropolitan's Flying Squad, Commander Kenneth Drury, went on a free holiday to Cyprus in the company of pornographer James Humphreys. It was alleged that in the West End certain police officers were receiving £1,000 a week in protection money from porn shops. Eventually fifteen officers were tried at the Old Bailey on corruption charges.

Worse still, in 1978 Operation Countryman was established to clean up alleged corruption in the Metropolitan Robbery Squad, the successor to the Flying Squad, which inherited the latter's flamboyant image, hand-made squad cuff-links and ties, and epic drinking sessions. The allegations were that some officers had moved from employing the illegitimate tactic of setting up robberies to catch unwitting villains, to actively planning and sharing in the proceeds of payroll robberies such as those at the *Daily Mirror* and the *Daily Express*. Heading the inquiry was Arthur Hambleton, Chief Constable of Dorset. The Countryman inquiries went beyond the original robberies—corruption in London appeared endemic and the team was expanded to over 100 officers. Yet in 1982 they were ordered to hand over their evidence to the Metropolitan's own investigation team. Hambleton retired, making public his belief that there was evidence on which to charge at least twenty-five officers. By August 1982 only nine had been charged and only two convicted. On ITV's *World in Action* that month, Hambleton said that the inquiry had been obstructed not merely by Scotland Yard but also by the office of the Director of Public Prosecutions, who had only agreed to four prosecutions from the first twenty-one submitted to it by the Countryman team.

While it would be absurd to deny the value of specialization, it is an organizational trend which threatens the old nature of policing as a service, and elevates the importance of crime as the central *raison d'être* of policing. It makes the police into authorities, the 'experts' of the 1980s; public debate invariably includes police representatives, not only when the topic is crime and justice but also in discussions on sexual morality, industrial relations, or terrorism.

The Police Powers War

The new professionalism also shows itself in the police's increased effectiveness as a political pressure group. The ability of the police to influence legislation has a long history—the swingeing powers granted by the Metropolitan Police Act, 1839 were the result of pressure from the Commissioners. More recently the introduction of majority verdicts in the 1967 Criminal Justice Act was a Home Office response to the police perception that a small number of 'professional' criminals were manipulating the jury system. But a major landmark in the history of criminal procedure was the 1984 Police and Criminal Evidence Act (PACE). It provided for the first time a coherent code of pre-trial practice for the police instead of an amalgam of powers and duties spread over case-law and statute. But, more important still, the police acquired many of the increased powers which they (and in particular Metropolitan Commissioner David McNee) had been demanding—the power to stop and search people on the street without the need to arrest; enhanced powers of arrest; the right to set up roadblocks; increased powers of detention. It was a triumph for the police establishment as a lobby force. It was also the last nail in the coffin of the idea that the constable was merely a citizen in uniform—the entire statute treats the uniformed officer as having powers peculiar to the office.

The statute grew out of the Royal Commission on Criminal Procedure (RCCP) set up under James Callaghan and reported in 1981 during the Thatcher administration. Its origins, paradoxically, lay in civil-liberties fears about police brutality, especially in the wake of the Confait case in 1972 when four youths were convicted of murder largely on the basis of their confessions. Several years later these

convictions were quashed by the Court of Appeal and in 1977 the
Fisher Report into the incident indicted the police officers who had
interrogated and extracted confessions from the youths.[4] But after the
political landscape changed beyond recognition in 1979 with the
Tory election success, the RCCP gave very little comfort to
libertarian critics. The parameters of the debate and of the recommendations themselves were set by Home Office civil servants who,
though willing to cede increased powers to the police, also wished to
build in substantial checks. The police argued that the increase in
crime levels and decrease in detection rates were the result of a
constricting definition of police powers. Yet Home Office research[5]
had found no evidence that increased powers would in any way have
this effect.

In many cases the powers requested were already being exercised
de facto by the police—black youth in London would testify to the
exercise of stop-and-search 'powers' for twenty years before PACE
and these were as bitterly resented as the 'move on' command in the
nineteenth century. Many defendants were held in police stations
'helping the police with their enquiries' without arrest or charge.
Perhaps the Home Office felt that the documentation detailing 'the
when, where, and how' of the exercise of these new powers would in
some measure control their exercise—already the custody record on
which the details of a defendant's detention are entered figures
largely in the trial, especially on the issue whether to admit the
defendant's statements into evidence. Even these safeguards, modest
when set alongside the new powers, have come under attack from the
police—in Greater Manchester in January 1987 senior officers were
citing the introduction of PACE as the reason for the rise in crime in
the city. They neglected to point out that the PACE powers had been
granted on the basis that they were essential to the task of reducing
crime rates.

There were other safeguards—the tape-recording of interrogations
was to be made nationwide; there was to be a system of duty solicitors
at all police stations so that a suspect could always have ready and
prompt access to legal advice; finally, the powers of prosecution that
the police had exercised for decades were to be taken away and vested
in the new Crown Prosecution Service which should provide an
independent check on the validity of prosecutions being pursued by
the police.

But despite these restrictions the police gained a significant prize in the stamp of legitimacy for temporary detention on the street and for lengthy periods in police stations. The power to detain another person physically is the most significant in civil society, one which citizens possess only in extreme cases. The State arrogates a much broader power to itself and delegates the exercise of it to the police. The fundamentals of liberal democracy require straightforward limits on that power—there should be clear conditions as to when and how it is exercised and a primary condition must be that serious harm has been done or is likely to be done.

These limits are axiomatic to the 'rule of law'. In the nineteenth century there was much greater adherence to the technical requirements of pre-trial procedure in arrest and charge. Investigation was not the job of the police. Suspects were not interrogated and constables were known to testify that the defendant had sought to make a statement, 'but I knew my duty and bade him be silent'. Constables are no longer bound by such rigid rules—instead they have a discretion to investigate based on 'reasonable suspicion' and interrogation is a major form of that investigation. In court the only question asked is whether it was reasonable for the constable to suspect the defendant and therefore to detain and search him. The quality of 'reasonableness' is so diffuse that a defendant will rarely challenge it in court, although in the heat of a dispute suspects may well deny an officer's right to intervene; but on the street the constable has the final say, through arrest for nebulous offences such as obstruction or breach of the peace.

According to the tenets of a 'liberal society', policing remains acceptable only when the police possess carefully defined legal powers to interfere. The process of generalizing their powers, and then of making such powers rest on the officer's discretion, removes a central constraint. What PACE and the Public Order Act 1986 provide is a cloak of legitimacy for their discretionary actions and policies, enabling them to intervene when and where they see fit—extraordinary powers for an autonomous and non-accountable public agency.

The Limits of Violence

Expanding their legal arsenal has had a parallel in the police capacity to use force. The traditional lack of weaponry among the police is not

an English eccentricity—initially and superficially it represented
Peel's attempt to distinguish the New Police from the military, but
on a deeper level it meshed with the prohibition on the arbitrary use
of physical force by the State, a key concept of liberalism. For many,
'freedom' means the knowledge that they are exempt from unjustified detention, pain, maiming, or death inflicted by the State. Police
abuse of an individual's body acquires an importance over and above
the injuries inflicted: deaths caused by police action or allegations
of assault attract massive attention when compared, for instance,
with injuries to mental patients by nurses or to prisoners by warders.

Injuries to officers (or their deaths in the course of their duties) are
deemed even more newsworthy. In 1986 the death, six years after the
original injuries, of PC Olds, shot in the course of a robbery,
commanded headlines in every newspaper. The same year saw corres-
pondence in the *Guardian* from social workers pointing out the risk
of assault run by social workers compared with the police. Yet murders of social workers by their clients are not 'news' compared with
the manhunts mounted after a policeman has been killed. Even the
death of a constable in a traffic accident will merit a paragraph in the
national press.

An attack on a constable has a range of overtones—policing as a
hazardous profession; the limits of 'respect' for law and the
uncivilized chaos that lurks beneath; the monopoly on the use of
'legitimate' force that is delegated to the police. But the police max-
imize their unparalleled access to the media to present every dead
police officer and every funeral in dramatic terms so as to present an
image of a beleaguered force, barred from 'no-go' areas or able to
patrol only in pairs, thus justifying demands for increasing resources
and greater armoury. The immediate result of the Brixton disturbances in 1981 was a reassessment not of the quality of policing in the
inner cities but of the need for riot shields, gas, and baton rounds.

While assaults by (as opposed to on) the police are less visible and
do not command the same degree of attention, they are still treated
with more significance than ordinary assaults—the names of Peach,
Waldorf, Kelly, Towers still haunt the police. In January 1983 Colin
Roach walked into Stoke Newington police station. A few minutes
later he was found dead from ·inshot wounds in the lobby. Two
months later a large public demonstration, protesting against the
insensitive and unsatisfactory police investigation, was violently

dispersed in Hackney by the police. In the absence of a satisfactory solution (normally a trial but perhaps an inquest or inquiry), the victims linger as ghosts in the public imagination, often building up resentment against the police. In Stoke Newington the deaths of Aseta Sims in 1971, Michael Ferreira in 1978, and Vivian Usherwood in 1980 all contributed to a history of suspicion and hostility.[6]

The failure to prosecute any of the SPG officers involved in the death of Blair Peach in Southall in April 1979 has been a continuing embarrassment to the Metropolitan force, whereas recently the prosecution and acquittal of the officers involved in the Waldorf, John Shorthouse, and Cherry Groce shootings meant a conclusive end to these episodes. These are exceptions: the vast majority of assaults or deaths through police action do not attract lasting attention or remedy. But when attention is focused on an act, a key issue should be whether minimum force was in fact employed. What has clearly occurred over the past decade has been a radical redefinition of what constitutes acceptable minimum force. A worrying statistic is the rise in the number of deaths in police custody: from a low of eight in 1970, they had risen to forty-eight in 1978 and thirty-two in 1979.

This redefinition has been most noticeable in public-order situations, discussed in detail in Chapter 5. The police have responded to the mass picket, demonstration, or meeting by 'mass policing', matching the number of demonstrators by an equal number of officers, frequently arrayed in riot gear and in military formation. Often they have an immediate goal, not necessarily connected with keeping order at all, such as enabling workers who are not on strike to enter the factory or mine or, as with *The Times* dispute at Wapping, allowing the distribution lorries to enter and leave. A less direct but more significant purpose is the exhibition of government muscle, reflecting a willingness on the part of the police authorities to reinforce political authority by coercive means, even within peacetime society. Mass policing denies recognition to civil liberties and is a dangerous innovation—a liberal/democratic constitution can only be upheld when those liberties are recognized and adhered to, especially by the police.

Secondly, while many specialist units are routinely armed—notably the drugs, robbery, and diplomatic protection squads and many SPG-type units—weapons are regularly issued to ordinary officers in a manner unknown before. Although Lee Enfield rifles were used in the siege of Sydney Street in 1911, until 1964 police stations would have only a limited stock of weapons, mainly .38 Webleys, for use in emergencies, defined as self-defence—facing a person who is armed. From 1966 the police started buying surplus army rifles and in 1971 the Galbraith Report (on the police use of firearms in peacetime) recommended the replacement of the Lee Enfields and Webleys—the Smith and Wesson is now the normal handgun used by the police.

The 1981 Home Office Guidelines state that weapons should be issued with the authorization of a senior officer when 'there is reason to suppose that a police officer may have to face a person who is armed or otherwise so dangerous that he could not safely be restrained without the use of firearms'. Clearly the police cannot be subjected to unnecessary risks. But the increasing number of occasions on which weapons are issued shows a dilution of earlier policies which carries substantial dangers. These are not only to the general public (revealed by the accidental shooting of 5-year-old John Shorthouse by a West Midlands officer searching a house, or of Cherry Groce in Brixton) but also to the police themselves. Deaths of police officers in the course of their duties are fortunately rare, and consistently arming the police is more likely to encourage an armed suspect to shoot (in supposed self-defence). Deaths of both officers and citizens are much more common in countries where the police are regularly armed. In England, on average one policeman a year has been murdered over the last twenty years. This compares with an average of four in West Germany, seven in France, and eighty-nine in the USA. Despite his unarmed status, the British police officer is the least likely to be the victim of a homicide.

Police armouries have increased in size and sophistication over the past two decades—Manwaring-White's survey shows that the firearms include, as well as handguns, rifles such as the high-velocity sniper rifle made by Lee Enfield, the Parker-Hale .222, or the Heckler-Koch .223, which gives an explosive-wound capacity similar to that of a dum-dum bullet. Three Nottinghamshire patrol cars have pump-action shotguns in a locked compartment and Manchester Chief Constable James Anderton in 1981 acquired Heckler-Koch HK 33 sub-machine-guns for use by his force. Before President Reagan's visit to Britain in 1984, twelve Metropolitan officers were trained to use a similar weapon. Heathrow is patrolled daily by officers with sub-machine-guns. Yet the only reason for such weapons is to spray whole areas: in what conceivable situation would this be necessary? But as well as firepower, the police can today call upon CS gas (used for the first time in Toxteth in 1981), rubber and plastic bullets, and water cannon.

Many London detectives always carry a gun, and in Nottingham, Hampshire, and the West Yorkshire cities of Leeds and Bradford patrol cars often have a locked compartment with a handgun. The number of occasions on which weapons have been issued has risen consistently from the early 1970s: in 1970 guns were issued on 1,072 occasions; in 1979 the figure had risen to 8,374; but in 1983 the Home Office decided to issue statistics only on the number of times guns were drawn—2,230 in 1983 and 1,838 in 1984. It is impossible to know how many police guns are on the streets at any time, although the increase in the issue of weapons is mainly in the London police divisions.

In the wake of public disquiet over the series of shooting accidents, the Home Office set up a working party which reported in February 1987 and recommended a new policy to encourage forces to set up specialist firearm units such as D11, the Metropolitan's Blue Berets who organize firearms training but also attend major shooting incidents. Fewer officers would be authorized to carry guns—the figure has dropped already from 10 per cent of the force in 1984 to 10,224 (8.6 per cent) in 1985, and the new policy would reduce this further. In London in 1983 4,776 of the force's 25,000 officers were 'authorized shots'—it is now intended to reduce this to 3,000.

The number of occasions on which such weapons are fired is still small—in the 1970s guns were discharged on only 20 occasions, causing 6 deaths and 5 injuries. In 1980–5 there were 40 incidents in which the police fired shots, resulting in 14 injuries and 2 deaths. Compared with other countries, guns are still used rarely in mainland Britain, but as more police officers are routinely armed this is unlikely to remain the case. Even given the small number of incidents, examples of the unnecessary use of police firearms abound. The public are at greater proportionate risk from armed policemen than the police are from members of the public. In 1982 a BBC TV documentary, *Police*, showed how one unconfirmed sighting of a man with a gun led to a house being surrounded with armed officers for hours until the suspect (a drunk sleeping it off) appeared, unarmed, at the door in the morning, only to be forced to the ground with some violence. No charges were ever brought. In a sense the man was lucky—had he been carrying a walking-stick, he might well have been shot.

In recent years Stephen Waldorf, John Shorthouse, and Cherry Groce have all been shot though unarmed and innocent of any offence. In June 1980 Gail Kinchin, 16 years old and pregnant, was held hostage by her boyfriend, Pagett. As he tried to leave the flat, using Gail as a shield, she was shot and killed by officers on the stairs who made no attempt to retreat. No officer was disciplined. Pagett was convicted of Gail's manslaughter. Even armed criminals should not forfeit their lives—even here 'minimum force' should mean self-defence. Three deaths (those of Basharat Hussain and Mohammed Hanif Hussain in February 1973 and of a bank robber in 1984) and at least two injuries have occurred when the 'weapon' was a plastic replica. Questions still remain over the death in 1978 of Michael Calvey, shot in the course of an armed robbery at a supermarket in Eltham—though armed, no shots were fired at the police and he was shot in the back. In February 1987, Dennis Bergin was shot by the Metropolitan police at the Sir John Soane Museum in Lincoln's Inn—though Bergin was armed, again no shots were fired at the police.

Although there is a need for some officers to be trained in the use of firearms, there is little justification for training a high proportion, for issuing weapons more frequently, or for maintaining firearms units on a permanent basis. The justification is not to be found in any 'crime' problem—although the statistical evidence shows an increase in offences involving firearms, the vast majority of this increase concerns the use of air weapons by juveniles. Nor, in more serious offences such as armed robbery, is there any evidence that arming the police prevents injuries to the police, prevents offences, or assists in the detection of the offenders.

4

Crimefighters?

Crime and Social Order

Policing is about crime: in the public view the main role of the police is controlling criminal behaviour. Failure to do so brings criticism. A string of burglaries provokes local questions, a stalled murder investigation leads to national editorials. This is not just the view of outsiders—internally the police also see themselves as 'crimefighters'. The 'good cop' makes arrests for 'proper' offences, catching burglars rather than speeding motorists. Worthwhile convictions enhance an officer's promotion and career prospects.

Institutionally the police use the crime statistics to press their arguments for increased resources—personnel, legal powers, or weaponry and computing services. Crime figures are certainly rising—in 1986, 3.8 million notifiable offences were recorded, over 7,650 for each 100,000 of the population. In 1957 the figure was 1,283 and in the 1930s it was as low as 350. But while these statistics provide the police with powerful arguments, they can also be used to show that recorded crime has actually risen coextensively with the increase in the police establishment. Does this mean that the police are ineffective or inefficient in controlling crime? In fact the general question, 'What, if anything, can the police do about it?' is never publicly asked. Before it can be asked, there are prior questions about the nature of 'crime' itself.

Over the last decade the politicians' debate on 'law and order' has observed strict limits. Crime is regarded as straightforward, since the official criminal statistics purport to measure how much crime there is and who is committing it. These figures do not treat the 'crime problem' as the behaviour of individuals but generalize it into a tangible entity, 'crime', about which we know facts, hold opinions, and form attitudes. The police and conservative politicians dominate the debate, supported by the newspapers' heavy reliance on a diet of crime stories—though their prurience is well concealed by a disingenuous censorious distaste. The assumptions are that crime is a major social problem, justifying attention and resources; that it reflects a malaise in our social structure, especially a lack of respect for authority engendered by school and family; that social and economic deprivation are less to blame than individual personality (moral failing rather than psychological disorder); and that the solution is more and better demonstrations of social authority—more discipline in schools and in the home, stronger policing, stiffer sentencing by judges, and harsher prison conditions, preferably with a return to capital and corporal punishment.

A growing body of research, not least from the Home Office itself, suggests that this orthodoxy is misplaced. Social obedience does not simply follow increased authoritarian measures. Yet many politicians who would agree with this view are wary of even entering the debate, primarily because to be seen to be 'soft' on crime is regarded as electoral suicide. The law-and-order card played a significant part in the Tory election victory of 1979, aided in part by the Police Federation who in the week before the election spent £21,000 on advertisements in the national newspapers with proposals which paralleled those of the Conservatives. Socialist and Liberal politicians content themselves with reformist measures, advocating ideas such as greater police accountability, shorter sentencing patterns, or prison reform. In the 1987 election, the Labour platform on 'crime' became more orthodox than the Conservative one, stressing high crime rates, the failure of the government to deal with it, and the desirability of more resources for the police with the sole *quid pro quo* of greater accountability. In practice, political parties of all persuasions are reluctant when in power to loosen the reins of social control.

There is a different, and less cynical, explanation of the gap between the crude approach of the 'law-and-order' brigade and modern research which casts doubt on the criminal justice enterprise, from the efficacy of police or prisons to the nature of 'crime' itself. Although public anxieties about crime appear on the surface to be manipulated by politicians and the media, they may spring from a deep common concern about personal security and the protection of private territory. In the edifice of the criminal justice system we provide ourselves with a symbol of reassurance that we are engaged in communal 'self-defence', and this reassurance is necessary, whether or not the system is effective in countering threats and whether or not the threats really exist.

That issue is beyond the immediate scope of this study, but it is worth asking what 'liberal philosophy' has to say about what constitutes crime and which people can be defined as criminals. To call an act a crime imbues it with a collective interest, distinct from the unregulated freedom of the private domain. How do we identify that interest? Let us take two examples—if someone takes another's property we call it theft and subject the thief to considerable sanctions, even imprisonment. But if someone fails to keep a promise to buy or sell or to perform a service, this leads not to punishment but to compensation for breach of contract. The effect on the victim can be identical, yet on the one hand we punish and stigmatize while on the other we merely compensate. In similar vein, we do not criminalize the manufacturer of cigarettes, although there are at least 50,000 nicotine-related deaths a year in the United Kingdom alone (a figure which tobacco companies aim to maintain and expand through advertising or sports sponsorship), but the heroin supplier is criminalized and may be tried for manslaughter.

How do we establish consistent criteria for deciding whether to treat an action as criminal? There is a preceding problem—why do we deal in the conceptual currency of crime at all? 'Crime' is not a natural concept. As was suggested in Chapter 2, wrongs between individuals do not inevitably need the resources of the community to resolve them. The idea that certain wrongs required extraordinary legal treatment was mainly an Angevin innovation under Henry II, when the State began to claim a public interest in private wrongs. At that time the king's objectives were not the improvement of the moral tone of the country but the establishment of a solid political base with authority centred firmly on the king, limiting the destabilizing tendencies of the provincial barons. The language of crime has always been useful in embodying political authority—colonial powers often enact criminal codes, such as Macaulay's Indian Penal Code (written in the 1830s and exported to many other British possessions), as a means of social and political control. They proscribe certain kinds of activity that a governing power finds harmful or disruptive, but are also necessary public demonstrations of social and political power. Trial and punishment are critical symbols of this, especially when they make the body the object of punishment, whether through execution, maiming, or imprisonment.

The discourse of 'crime' and 'law and order' is as much about power as it is about good and evil. In Chapter 8 I will argue that a central liberal theme is how to control sovereign power. When linked to the stress on individual freedom, 'crime' in liberal philosophy would be narrowly circumscribed. A 'collective' interest would have to be clearly identified and given priority only where the majority agrees that it is absolutely necessary. Very few crimes might remain on the statute book: assault or theft could in theory be essentially a private affair, whereas serious violence or killing do pose threats to the cohesion of the community as a whole—societies which did not protect their members from such harms would be short-lived.

This narrow formulation of the concept of 'crime' does not represent the modern basis of the criminal law, which punishes a wide range of acts which threaten personal security, personal property, or public comfort—it is the petty thieves, drunks, and vagrants who form the staple diet of the courts. Thus the criminal justice system is the vehicle for broad state intervention. A justification for such breadth comes from Devlin,[1] who argues that even the most private aspects of a life, such as homosexuality, can undermine the sexual and family relationships which form a natural moral basis of social order. Such lifestyles could presage radical change against which a society has a right to protect itself. A parallel argument could be advanced about the protection of property rights against theft and deception—the market economy would be destabilized without the reinforcement and affirmation of the importance of private property through the punishment of thieves.

These broader definitions of crime leave no boundaries to the potential scope of the criminal law. What aspects of a person's behaviour or even thought do not have wider implications for society? Though this need provide no problem for an authoritarian, the liberal still searches for boundary lines: one traditional restriction is the requirement for proof of direct harm to an individual's property or person, but even here problems abound—when does a direct infringement of economic interests (theft or breach of contract) cease to be a private matter and become of concern to the State? Should two youths be legally entitled to agree to fight in public?

Are there clear legal or ethical criteria on which we criminalize behaviour? Or can these questions about crime only be answered in terms of social power? If so, the function of the criminal justice system is straightforward authoritarian control of other people's actions, and 'liberal' speculation on such questions has a hint of futility. Any survey of the modern criminal law reveals its all-embracing scope and distinctive lack of boundaries, and it becomes clear that the way criminal definitions are imposed is a measure of political authority: in the eighteenth century the expansion of commerce and banking meant equivalent creativity in the criminal law, with new offences of fraud and embezzlement; the demonstrations and strikes of the 1970s have brought a Public Order Act, redefining old offences and creating new ones with the intention further to invalidate political and industrial dissent.

Liberal philosophy is bereft in the face of power exercised through parliamentary democracy—it was constitutionally agreed that both poor and rich were forbidden to steal bread or sleep under bridges. The inequalities of social and economic power are more significant than idealist philosophies in labelling behaviour as criminal or in enforcing the laws, although in the area of enforcement the liberal critique has a much more practical role to play.

That critique asserts fundamentally that laws must be enforced equally, neutrally, and universally. Yet surveys of the courts or prisons show that some social groups are much more vulnerable to arrest and prosecution than others. Young working-class males, particularly if they are black, are more likely to appear in criminal courts than other groups. This is not because these individuals are society's criminals—self-report studies show that serious harmful behaviour is spread more or less evenly across the population (even white, middle-class, middle-aged widows commit offences). Sometimes real direct harm is not formally defined as crime or, when it is technically criminal, it is not subject to the same rigorous scrutiny and enforcement. In 1987 the insider trading scandal which followed the Guinness takeover bid for Distillers was only revealed by US security exchange officials investigating another matter. The Guinness directors, who resigned or were dismissed, could have faced lesser sentences, had they been prosecuted, than a domestic burglar.

Pointing to the prevalence of harmful acts or the inequalities of law enforcement does not make crime disappear—there are acts of violence and exploitation which require collective response. But we transform our response into social drama, constantly displaying the 'fragility' of order, the 'need' to protect individuals against the depredations of others, and the necessity to accept social authority as provider of that protection. The players in the drama change slowly—the football hooligan or the mugger have garrotters as their nineteenth-century predecessors; while we regard cannabis or heroin as the modern anti-social drug, for the eighteenth century and Hogarth it was gin. There is an arbitrary quality about these targets—only a few are chosen as examples; the harm inflicted is often minimal, especially in comparison with other non-criminal activities; the crude brutality of the penal approach seems wholly inappropriate when alternative approaches would bear more fruit. All this suggests that the content of our criminal drama appears to have little importance—the sub-plot emphasizes the importance for the audience of coherence and solidarity against outsiders and enemies and, even more striking, the form of the play, especially in the courtroom scenes, expresses social patterns of authority and deference.

In maintaining the significance of the 'crime problem', the police have institutional interests of their own. To ensure that public resources are channelled into the 'law-and-order' budget they need to show the public an identifiable 'crime problem'. This is ready-made in the quantifiable and 'scientific' criminal statistics. But through their Annual Reports, advertising campaigns, and press briefings, Chief Constables also deal in more discursive images which feed our beliefs in the 'reality' of crime and what it consists of—the mugger and the unsafe streets; the burglar wrecking a house; the drug peddler. Violence towards women in the home, racialist attacks, or income-tax evasion get scarcely any attention, either through enforcement or through publicity. Why do the police concentrate on particular areas and not on others? As I will argue in Chapter 6, the incidents which are ignored often reflect the accepted social authority of the male or the white man and pose no threat to traditional authority or to the market. It is a broad, inarticulated concept of tradition and authority that the police defend.

However, the rest of this chapter concerns the mechanics of the exercise of discovering and solving crime and the justifications for the police tag of 'crimefighters'.

Measuring Crime

It is a common-sense view that the amount of crime will vary according to the resources available to the police. It may be common sense,
but it is not true: more police do not necessarily bring about any
reduction in crime. Fundamentally the level of recorded crime
depends on the public rather than on the police, and so the absolute
level is unknowable. Thus it is impossible to state with any acceptable degree of precision whether crime rates are rising or falling.

First and foremost the police react to the public who 'discover'
offences and report them. Many everyday actions within the office,
factory, school, or home are 'potential' crimes and only a small sample
ever get discovered or reported. This means that there is a 'dark
figure' of unrecorded offences which can only be guessed at.
Sociologists suggest that overall one offence in four is ever known to
the police but this figure varies from offence to offence. In 1983 the
Home Office produced the first *British Crime Survey (BCS)*. Its
findings confirmed that if a car goes missing it will invariably be
reported to the police for insurance reasons and to speed recovery.
Conversely, only a small amount of shoplifting or stock loss will ever
be reported, and only when there is an identified offender. Only a
small proportion of rapes and sexual assaults is ever recorded, as
women are reluctant to report them, and only a minority of woundings are ever reported to the police.

People fail to report incidents for a variety of reasons and are
unlikely to report anything seen as 'normal', such as pilfering from
the workplace or a pub brawl. The relationship between victims,
offenders, and witnesses is also critical—the closer that relationship,
whether by blood, friendship, or job, the greater the tolerance of
behaviour that, were it committed by a stranger, would lead to calling
the police. This helps to explain the low proportion of assaults and
woundings that are reported—fights are frequently between acquaint-
ances, not to say friends and relatives, and the police would be
regarded as outsiders. The employment relationship also acts as protection—the secretary who is indecently assaulted by her boss is
unlikely to complain publicly for fear of losing her job. Even when
the act is seen as a crime it may not be reported, especially if it is felt
that the police could not do anything about it or would not be interested. Further, the victim might prefer to treat the matter as private—

banks, for example, are unwilling to court publicity by prosecuting embezzling bank clerks, and shops prefer to warn or sack employees caught stealing (then raising their prices to cover the costs of stock loss). Embarrassment may be a further reason for non-reporting especially in the areas of sexual assault and blackmail.

There may be positive reasons to go to the police—the recovery of stolen property; a preliminary step to making an insurance claim; protection from assault. Overall a picture of general reluctance to report offences would be inaccurate—people contact the police about a mass of trivial incidents. Of all the thefts and burglaries reported to the police, one-third will involve property valued at £5 or less.

What gets reported, let alone why, is a complex picture, but reporting is no guarantee of the next step, that it will be recorded by the police as a notifiable offence. The police record only one in three of cases of vandalism reported to them—the officer may listen politely, even make a note, but the incidents will be 'lost' or 'cuffed', simply because they are unlikely ever to be cleared up. The *BCS* found that only 70 per cent of burglaries reported to the police are recorded as such. (A caveat about such figures is that, while the public may call an incident a 'burglary', the police may quite legitimately describe it as 'theft in a dwelling'.) Significant numbers of 'robberies' may also be redefined as theft, while lesser assaults and minor thefts from the person often disappear altogether.

The Criminal Statistics reflect only what the police choose to record of what the public have chosen to report. It is a measure of public/police activity and not of any absolute level of criminal behaviour. Yet newspapers treat them as such—the *Guardian* in March 1987 headlined its report on the publication of the 1986 figures 'Rapes lead rise to record crime rate', even though the commentary below warned against reading statistics in this way. Tabloid papers are less particular. It is these statistics (and the press coverage of them) which feed, and often distort, perceptions about crime.

To take one example, from 1974 to 1984 the Criminal Statistics recorded an increase of 125 per cent in burglary—indeed, the years 1979–86 show a doubling in the number of domestic burglaries, from 250,000 to 500,000. But another canvass of domestic burglary, this time by the General Household Survey, revealed a much smaller rise, approximately 20 per cent, from 1974 to 1984. Such a difference can only be accounted for by assuming that the lower figure represents the actual rise in burglaries and the higher represents the rise in the reporting rate—as a result of, say, more domestic telephones, more house-contents insurance policies, the effect of advertising campaigns on crime prevention, and less antipathy towards the police.

Changes such as these can significantly affect statistics without any underlying change in the crime rate itself: the 1986 figures reveal a 9 per cent decrease in thefts from shops. Any conclusion that we are becoming more honest would be fatuous: the decline must be explained by shopkeepers and store detectives being less eager to report shoplifting to the police.

Similarly, the apparent rise in burglary does not necessarily mean greater vulnerability of the home, although this is the picture implied by the statistics. People's anxieties about burglary mirror this and often incorporate misleading stereotypes from 'crime-prevention' publicity. Burglary is assumed to occur at night, with a high level of damage to the property, confrontation between the owner and the burglar, and significant violence. Yet the 'typical' burglary is carried out in the owner's absence by a teenage male, portable items of low value are taken, violence and unnecessary damage are rare, and it is all over in a few minutes. The total cost of insurance claims following burglaries in 1983 was the relatively low figure of £110 million. There is a strange divergence between the image of burglary as a serious offence, attracting heavy sentences (85 per cent of burglars will receive custodial sentences), and the reality of the average burglary.

This example shows how difficult it is to know whether 'crime is on the increase'—a recent increase in rape reports in London (from 570 in 1985 to 824 in 1986) probably reflects a greater willingness of victims to report attacks, following a well-publicized introduction by the Metropolitan police of a 'softly, softly' approach to the questioning and treatment of rape victims, rather than an increase in the number of sexual assaults in London. It is undoubtedly safer not to use the Criminal Statistics as a basis for speculation on the moral economy of the country.

The counter-argument is that real and serious crime *is* measured by the Criminal Statistics and that the *BCS*, among others, includes a mass of trivia which would be weeded out by the police were it to come to their attention. The *BCS* does include small incidents (although it specifically excludes one million instances of threatening behaviour and the 10 per cent of households who suffer thefts of milk from their doorsteps), but many of those not reported to the police will have been quite serious—domestic and sexual assault and racialist attacks are clear examples. On the other hand, the Criminal Statistics themselves record a mass of trivial property offences. For example, 50 per cent of recorded burglaries involve property loss of under £25, and 75 per cent under £100. It has been estimated that the inmates of Pentonville are in prison for stealing on average £5. Minor incidents artificially inflate the statistics of serious offences—the total of firearms offences includes a high proportion of incidents involving children playing with airguns and causing criminal damage, and attendance at any juvenile court will produce absurd examples of children prosecuted for taking cakes or ringing doorbells.

Policing Crime

That the police are receivers and recorders of crime reports from members of the public means that they have limited control over input to their workload. But their operational policies also affect crime figures: where officers are deployed will affect what criminal offences are uncovered. To take a non-police example, the decision to increase the fraud investigation squads attached to the DHSS inevitably brings a rise in the number of fraudulent social security claims discovered. The reverse also applies: in the 1980s the reduced numbers of investigators attached to the Inland Revenue lessened the risk of discovery for tax evaders.

The police also have scope to focus their activities: the creation of drugs squads will lead to a rise in prosecutions for possession and supply; deploying officers in strength at demonstrations or on picket lines will lead to arrests for public-order offences. Whitaker[2] cites the example of the Manchester Chief Constable who ordered a crackdown on homosexuals frequenting public lavatories, leading to a rise of 1,000 per cent in prosecutions for indecency between males. These decisions are discretionary and are rarely questioned in Parliament or by Local Police Authorities, yet they inevitably affect the public perception of what the serious crime problems are. Occasionally there are criticisms from local communities about the lack of beat patrols, or more specific problems such as the failure of the Metropolitan Police to tackle racialist assault and arson in East London. In the main, operational decisions go unseen and unremarked.

However, the police's routine ability to go out and find crime is limited. On the beat the officer will rarely stumble over offences in progress. CID's normal work consists of reacting to crime reports, though there may be investigations initiated by regional crime squads or other specialist squads, targeting particular suspected offences or offenders.

What is the effect of officers on the beat? The public demand for increases in their number would only seem justified by a decrease in, say, street offences or burglary. The implications of recent research suggest the opposite: the greater accessibility through more beat officers would lead to a lowering of the threshold at which people consider a matter worth reporting.

One might expect patrolling to achieve a decrease in crime if there were sufficient officers in an area. But even here the studies have proved equivocal[3]—the visibility of the police, especially on foot, is important, but once there is at least one officer walking the beat, additional officers on the same beat seem to have little effect. There is also a displacement effect—although offences in the immediate area are reduced, there may be a corresponding increase in crime in neighbouring streets. Moreover, high levels of policing in a community can create considerable resentment through the inevitable interference with normal life.

While beat officers often encounter (or create) public-order offences, such as obstruction or threatening words or behaviour, it is rare that they encounter 'crime in progress'. An average foot beat in a city covers some 200 acres, 4 to 5 miles of public road, and a population of about 4,000. The chances of an officer stumbling across any incident are small. In the US in the 1960s the President's Commission on Law Enforcement and the Administration of Justice came to the conclusion that the average patrolling officer could expect to intercept a street robbery once every fourteen years. Similar conclusions could be drawn about officers encountering a burglary. The common-sense response would be to take officers from the beat and put them into cars: this would be the most effective way of getting manpower to the scene of the action as quickly as possible. Again common sense is a less than reliable guide—a project in Kansas City revealed that speed of police response did not necessarily lead to more arrests. The critical factor was that it takes on average about thirty minutes for a victim to report an incident—comfort and assistance are first sought from friends and relatives. Patrol cars do not lead to decreased crime rates, nor do they give the public the sense of reassurance that foot patrols do.

Policing is only partly about crime. The constable provides much wider services to the community. One of these is the reduction of fear of assault or burglary through physical presence. Ironically the police presentation of themselves as battling with a rising tide of crime is arguably the major source of this fear. But in the late twentieth century the fear of crime is as great a problem as crime itself. It is a fear that ties older people to their homes and leads to city centres being deserted at night. It is a fear that does not correspond to the actual risk of being a victim. The *BCS*'s calculations showed that a typical household might be burgled once every forty years; that you might be robbed once every 500 years and assaulted with slight injury once in geological time. Women, particularly those over 60, are most concerned about burglary, mugging, and sexual assault, and young men have the least anxiety—yet the young white male is the likeliest victim.

The risks of crime that we run are much less than a range of other risks—the risk of fire is greater than that of burglary; the risk of traffic injury greater than that of having your car taken; the risk of psychiatric illness greater than that of a mugging. These risks do not claim our attention in the same manner as crime. Of course, an assault or burglary is an invasion of your privacy by another person, and this is very different from damage by something impersonal, be it fire, illness, or a car on the road. The personal quality attacks deep-seated beliefs about relationships with others, in a way that an assault by an inanimate object such as a car can never do. The presence of the constable not only embodies the principle of the rule of law but underlines co-operative protection and is more effective in reducing anxieties than public education which provides information on the realistic assessment of risks.

Reassurance is delivered more effectively through the 'crime-fighter' image. One ingredient of this is direct confrontation with the offender, caught red-handed—the Wild West posse, the feudal hue-and-cry have their modern counterpart in 'hot pursuit'. How far should patrolling be organized to anticipate this possibility? Most offences are completed very quickly—the average robbery is over in 40 seconds and the likelihood of pursuit is minimal. Yet in

Manchester, Chief Constable James Anderton initiated an armed squad of policemen on the streets to combat a rise in armed robberies—sixty-four in 1982. A mistaken move, since it does not increase the chances of intercepting the robbers, while the arming of officers does increase the chance of causing injuries to others. The lesson of Detroit might have persuaded Manchester to adopt different tactics—there a STRESS squad (*S*Top *R*obberies *E*njoy *S*afe *S*treets) was disbanded after being involved in seventeen fatal shootings.

In this country the equivalent sheriff–outlaw ethos leads not to pulling guns but to high-speed car chases, less dramatic but equally fatal: eleven people were killed in police-car accidents in 1983 in London alone.[4] The toll has risen steadily in recent years, possibly as a result of the 1979 Road Traffic Act which specifically exempts emergency-service vehicles from observing speed limits or traffic lights. Yet often the car chase is a response to a trivial incident—in 1984 Simon Hansford was killed when being chased for not wearing a seat belt. Often the victims are uninvolved—in Oxford in 1982 an 18-year-old cyclist, Gregory Dixon, was hit head-on by a police transit van driving on the wrong side of the road and having gone through two sets of red lights. The driver was fined £100. In Birmingham in 1985 a family car was hit by a stolen car being chased by four police cars. The driver, Colin Webb, was killed and his wife and son had to be pulled from the burning vehicle while the police continued their 'hot pursuit'. This was in direct contravention of the Home Office manual which states that it is better to allow a criminal to escape than to endanger road users.

Despite this official policy, police drivers seem to be relatively immune from prosecution, severe punishment if convicted, or even internal disciplinary action. In 1985, 2,798 cases of serious accidents involving the police were reported to the Director of Public Prosecutions who advised criminal proceedings in only 695 cases, and by December 1986 there had been no known successful prosecutions.

Clearing Up Crime

If policing policy has only a limited effect on crime rates and the discovery of crime, how effective are the police in resolving crime by the arrest and prosecution of offenders? The most immediate index of effectiveness is the clear-up rate, which expresses offences solved to the satisfaction of the police as a percentage of crimes notified to them. The overall clear-up rate was approximately 31.6 per cent in 1986, having declined from 45 per cent in 1974. In that period, although the number of solved crimes increased, the overall number of offences notified to the police increased faster. The clear-up rate varies from offence to offence—in homicide the police are successful in over 90 per cent of cases. Indeed, seven in ten of most offences of violence, including sexual assault, are cleared up to the satisfaction of the police. But in burglary the national clear-up rate is only 22 per cent, although that can vary from force to force. Judicious redefining of a burglary as a theft from a dwelling can massage these figures into respectability. Manipulation can occasionally transgress the borders of the acceptable—in 1986–7 the Kent police force were investigated by the Police Complaints Authority when officers alleged that detectives were inducing prisoners to confess to offences they had not committed in order to bolster the detection rate.

We must distinguish the problem of the unidentified offender from those crimes which are solved at the same time that they are reported. Whole classes of crime come within this category and provide little guide to the effectiveness of the police. Shoplifting does not come to the attention of the police unless there is an offender apprehended by the store and ready to be processed. Handling stolen goods and fraud are similar—once a deception comes to light, so does the offender. Clear-up rates are thus artificially raised. In the Criminal Statistics the clear-up rate for the category of theft/handling drops from 35 to 24 per cent when shoplifting and handling are excluded.

The clear-up rate for offences against the person, from lesser assault to homicide, is a respectable 75 per cent. With such offences, typically the offender and victim are known to each other. In our imagination we fear assault at night by a stranger hiding in a dark alley. The reality, as Jessica Mitford[5] suggests, is that you are in much greater danger of personal violence sitting at home in your own armchair, surrounded by your 'loved' ones. Usually there is no problem of identification or resolution—96 per cent of attempted murders are solved. This is frequently the case, not merely with offences of violence, but with a range of other incidents. Even if the victim does not know the offender, the latter is often clearly identified by a witness or detained at the scene of the event by a uniformed officer or store detective. No problem of detection is involved.

Also important in the analysis of the clear-up rate are those offences 'taken into consideration' (TICs) by the court at trial. Although the offender is not charged with these offences at court, the judge may take them into consideration in assessing sentence for the offence charged. This operates as a bar to any further prosecution for these offences. For offenders it is a simple way of wiping the slate clean, though at the risk of some additional punishment. For the police, when a suspect admits other offences, it is a welcome boost to the clear-up rate. Approximately one offence in four is discovered and solved in this fashion. Again this varies from offence to offence— it is rare for an offender to ask for violent or sexual crimes to be taken into consideration; conversely, nearly 40 per cent of burglary cases are cleared up in this way. Offenders admit to long lists of previous offences: the Oxford Penal Research Unit discovered a defendant at a Sheffield court in the 1960s who had asked for over 1,000 additional offences to be taken into consideration. Here skill in interrogation becomes a crucial policing technique, as these previous offences will invariably be revealed during an interview.

An analysis of cleared-up offences conducted by Clarke and Hough[6] shows that in 26 per cent of cases the offender was still at the scene. In half of those cases the suspect was detained by a member of the public or a store detective. In the other half the arrest resulted from police observation or the defendant gave himself up. In a further 27 per cent of cases the offence was resolved by being taken into consideration at a subsequent court hearing. In 24 per cent of cases the suspect was detained as a result of information from the public, usually identifying the offender. In the remainder of cases, the arrest was more the result of the public's stereotype of police work—the use of informants, of special inquiries, of plants, or the vigilance of constables.

Sherlock Holmes is patently the wrong image for the modern CID —painstaking and detailed enquiries, forensic skill, and deductive reasoning are the exception rather than the rule in solving cases. Just as the public are responsible for the discovery and reporting of crime, so they also provide the answers. Clear-up rates do not rely on the police, who, crudely, might be said to be the recorders and processors of crime rather than its preventers and detectors. Morris[7] has suggested that figures such as these call into question the effectiveness of patrolling systems and of criminal investigation strategies. It would appear that nothing in the way of organization of staff or revision of procedures, either in uniformed patrolling or in CID, would materially affect clearance rates.

The exception may be the highly specific approach to crime problems: this was discussed in the previous chapter in relation to serious targeted offences, where concentration of resources can bring good results. This is shown by the successful conclusion of most homicide investigations. On a lesser level, crowd troubles at football matches can be reduced by liaison with clubs to ensure proper supervision and segregation of supporters as well as the development of 'members only' schemes such as that devised by Luton Town. Specialized patrolling—assigning officers to specific locations for the explicit purpose of controlling particular offences—may also improve crime control.

Results can flow from specifying clear objectives, but does policing have no effect on general crime levels? Can it be argued that the police operate under serious constraints which prevent them from being more effective in the 'war against crime'? In terms of resources, the police establishment has risen by 150 per cent since 1945. In the mid-nineteenth century the inspectors of constabulary sought a ratio of one constable to 1,000 citizens. Now that ratio approaches 1 : 400, and by March 1988 police establishment in England and Wales will be 124,363, having risen by 25 per cent since 1974. During the period 1979–85 the budget for police services rose from £1.1 billion to £2.8 billion. There are probably more patrolling officers than ever before. There is no evidence that any increase in resources leads to a decrease in the crime rate. The converse is true—more and more incidents get treated as criminal offences which before might have been dealt with informally, furthering the illusion of a spiralling crime rate, out of control.

From the mid-1960s the police have consistently argued that the legal rules of criminal procedure, both pre-trial and at the trial itself, hampered the detection and conviction of criminals. Robert Mark, in his time as Chief Constable of Leicestershire, successfully campaigned to abolish the centuries-long tradition of unanimity in the jury through the introduction by the Criminal Justice Act 1967 of the majority verdict. The attack on the jury system by the police has been unabated, fuelled in the early 1970s by Mark's Dimbleby Lecture

'Minority Verdict'. The recent target has been the defendant's right of peremptory challenge to jurors, once a right to challenge any juror but restricted to challenging three in 1977 and now likely to be abolished.

In pre-trial procedure, as was discussed in the previous chapter, the police have always sought to abolish the right to silence and to have more stringent powers, such as the legal right to stop individuals on the street without arresting them and to perform a limited search. These were put forward strongly to the Royal Commission on Criminal Procedure during its deliberations from 1979 to 1981. Many of these demands were met in the Police and Criminal Evidence Act 1984, although earlier research by Steer[8] suggested that no obvious additions to police powers were likely to increase police effectiveness in the prevention and detection of crime. These assertions are supported by the fact that the police already exercised, de facto, many of the powers now granted in the 1984 legislation. Stop and search without arrest was and is a common experience, especially among young males, not only blacks. What enables the police to act in this manner is that any incriminating material that they find (offensive weapons, drugs, stolen goods) will be admitted into evidence by the judge without comment on the manner in which it was obtained. There were no sanctions—the end justified the means. The suspect, once convicted, had little basis for bringing an action or lodging a complaint and those who were not arrested or charged would rarely have evidence for court proceedings and would probably judge the police complaints procedure to be of little value.

Steer's conclusions that additional powers would have no effect on the crime rate might be further supported by statistics from Manchester in October 1986 which show reported offences in Greater Manchester up by 16 per cent from January to June 1986, with the detection rate falling. Chief Constable Anderton now blames (a sentiment echoed by Commissioner Newman in London) the Police and Criminal Evidence Act for introducing bureaucratic procedures for dealing with prisoners (that is, a custody officer in each police station). The allegation is that this increases the hours spent on paperwork and thus reduces the number of officers available for street patrol. Such an analysis is interesting, as it goes against much of the evidence considered in this chapter. It again shows the high political profile of senior officers—the high crime rate had previously been used before the Royal Commission on Criminal Procedure to justify increased police powers. The powers are introduced, the crime rates still increase, and so the argument is changed, on the one hand to attack the safeguards which were put into the legislation to counterbalance the increased powers, and on the other, to focus on a new target—the suspect's right of silence, abolition of which was proposed at the 1987 Conservative Conference by Home Secretary Douglas Hurd, despite the fundamental change that this would make to the burden of proof in criminal cases.

The numbers, organization, and powers of the police do not affect the discovery, reporting, and resolution of crime as materially as the public believes. The Home Office recognizes this: the new police/public consultative committees set up under PACE are to educate the public in the limits of what the police can and cannot do. There are serious offences where labour-intensive investigations produce results—though as the prosecution of Peter Sutcliffe, the Yorkshire Ripper, showed, sometimes more from luck and an observant and quick-witted officer. But police forces themselves are also down-grading whole categories of criminal investigation such as burglary and car theft—no further action will be taken when a preliminary assessment suggests a low possibility of success. Ironically, if the last twenty years have seen heightened expectations from the public about police capabilities, and thus an apparent rise in crime rates, the increasing awareness that the police will do nothing about certain offences will lead to a decline in reporting rates—and so to an apparent decrease in 'crime' itself.

5

The Police and Public Order

Introduction

Over the last fifteen years the police have constantly confronted strikers and demonstrators—the scale and diversity of protests have been unprecedented since the first half of the nineteenth century which witnessed Peterloo, the Luddites, Captain Swing, Chartism, and the Rebecca riots. The contemporary record includes political demonstrations the dispersal of which led to deaths of demonstrators at Red Lion Square in 1974 or at Southall in 1979; pitched battles in cities in both 1981 and 1985—St Paul's in Bristol, Brixton, Toxteth, Broadwater Farm; disorder in sports grounds, particularly at football matches—the notorious Luton v. Millwall match in 1985 came only weeks before the Heysel stadium tragedy in Brussels; anti-nuclear protests, especially by the peace women at Greenham Common, who have been the object of constant police attention; the well-publicized police 'riot' which attacked the Peace Convoy seeking to celebrate the solstice at Stonehenge in 1985.

But the confrontational mass policing of industrial disputes has attracted the most controversy. Control by confrontation can be dated from the closure of the Saltley coking works by a mass picket of miners in 1972. The police saw this as a 'defeat' and developed strategies to ensure future police 'victories'. This determination to beat mass picketing has been shown at the dispute over union recognition at Grunwicks in 1977, the miners' strike over the National Coal Board plans for the industry during 1984–5, and the NGA lockout by Rupert Murdoch and *The Times* over the introduction of new technology at Wapping in 1986–7.

Concern about public order has grown, primarily centred on the considerable violence, throwing paving stones or petrol bombs and attacking police officers, one of whom, PC Keith Blakelock, was stabbed to death in Tottenham in 1985. The press as a whole condemned these disturbances as 'meaningless' or 'criminal'. Yet each had its own unique history, and public concern has focused, among an amalgam of 'causes', on the recurring theme of hostility to the police, generated by the tactics employed, by the prior policing of neighbourhoods, or by the police handling of particular incidents—when Clinton McCurbin was arrested in Wolverhampton in February 1987 on suspicion of using a stolen credit card, it was with such force that he died of asphyxia. That night, mounted police were needed to disperse crowds protesting at his death. Reports and inquiries relating to such incidents have proliferated and juries have even refused to convict on riot charges in both Sheffield and Bristol. It has now become clear that there is as much concern about the tactics of policing crowds as there was about public disorder.

Some of the gatherings of these past few years were not even potentially violent, yet the hippies at Stonehenge attracted hundreds of riot police. The most innocuous demonstration will have a full quota of constables, often outnumbering the demonstrators—during the teachers' industrial action in 1987 an open-air meeting in a park by the Imperial War Museum attracted not only a substantial police presence but a further three busloads of officers in reserve. Can there really have been such an apprehension of disorder?

Of course a major police task has always been to scrutinize and regulate crowds. Unlike 'crime control' the demands of the job are obvious, but whereas criminal justice is subject to relatively specific rules and procedures, the management of public order relies much more on the discretionary and subjective language of 'reasonable apprehension', 'public interest', or 'breach of the peace'. The objective of managing crowds dominates over collective rights and that objective is assumed to justify wide police interference with any gathering.

Individual and Collective Rights

Legally, public 'rights', whether individual or collective, rest on a fragile surface: they are residuary rather than positive freedoms. For instance, the right of assembly and meeting in public is subject to a range of possible offences (not least, obstruction of the highway), and there is no positive right to use the road or public space for anything other than passing and repassing and reasonable rest and recreation. Nor are there 'public' buildings with rights of access for public meetings: prospective speakers find themselves constrained by the private ownership of halls or lecture theatres.

Although we believe in fundamental liberties of assembly and speech, they have no constitutional or legal protection and judges have consistently avoided deciding such issues. In 1936 in *Duncan* v. *Jones*, Lord Hewart (who had been a journalist and a liberal MP and was Attorney-General in Lloyd George's Liberal Government before becoming Lord Chief Justice) encountered Mrs Duncan, who had wished to talk about the Incitement to Disaffection Bill on the steps of New Cross Unemployed Training Centre. A constable had suggested that she move around the corner and, when she refused, had arrested her for obstructing a constable in the execution of his duty. The court might have argued that freedom of speech was too important to be impeded without serious cause. It did not, and instead took the narrow view that the case was about the scope of a constable's duty—it was sufficient that he had acted lawfully, and no wider issue needed to be invoked. In a classic statement of the common law's position, Lord Hewart said:

There have been moments during the argument in this case when it appeared to be suggested that the Court had to do with a grave case involving what is called the right of public meeting. I say 'called' because English law does not recognise any special right of public meeting for political or other purpose. . . The case, however, does not even touch that important question.

Courts rarely interfere with the exercise of police powers, and in public these powers severely affect individuals' rights: the basic liberal freedoms are curtailed. Pedestrians can be stopped and searched (under s. 1 Police and Criminal Evidence Act); vehicles and their drivers are subject to similar provisions, and drivers have to produce driving licences and other documents as well as follow the instructions of an officer. Making speeches, handing out pamphlets, selling newspapers or other goods, collecting money for a cause, Morris dancing, or playing guitars—all are at the discretion of the police.

This discretion inevitably puts individual rights under some stress. But for crowds, 'rights' scarcely exist at all. As suggested already, to use the road or any other public space for meetings, speeches, or sales would, *prima facie*, constitute the criminal offence of obstruction and be subject to a battery of other police powers at common law and under the Public Order Acts of 1936 and 1986. The latter gives the police power to move pickets, re-site mass assemblies, and re-direct marches; organizers of a march have to give six days' notice and provide a detailed route map. It also gives the police a new ground for intervention: serious disruption to the life of a community. Intervention is based not on the 'letter of the law' but on more ambiguous criteria: a reasonably grounded apprehension of a 'breach of the peace' entitles them to disperse gatherings or to arrest. But 'breach of the peace', let alone its 'reasonable apprehension', is very vague—does it require a person to become violent? Or someone to be offended by abusive language? Or traffic to be disrupted? Or an innocent bystander to be put in fear? The officer's judgement is central and this makes it difficult to challenge *ex post facto*.

These broad discretionary powers highlight the paradox of strict control co-existing with collective freedoms, of speech, meeting, and protest, that patently exist and yet seem almost illusory. In 1984, for example, miners heading north through the Blackwall Tunnel from Kent to Nottingham found themselves turned back by officers apprehending a breach of the peace which was to happen some hundreds of miles away. Yet the NUM took no legal steps against what was, technically, a clear abuse of police power. Section 14 of the new Public Order Act enabled the police in June 1987 to 'move on' hippies parked on a Wiltshire farm track because they were a 'disruptive influence'.

With crowds the police are free to use their subjective judgement. The fear of 'disorder' is easily alleged and impossible to disprove. Furthermore, there are no entrenched collective rights to meet, picket, or protest. Linked to the width and vagueness of police powers, the crowd is, not surprisingly, regarded, if not as illegal, then as on the borders of illegality. Marches and meetings, and anyone engaging in them, are seen as having the potential for violence, either to people or to property, and thus deserve police suspicion and attention. Throughout 1986/87, the constant dispersals and arrests on the picket line outside South Africa House have been justified by the 'possibility' of offences, a possibility which overrides the right to protest peacefully. In the 1984 Metropolitan

Commissioner's report, public demonstrations were significantly placed alongside burglaries as the major problems that the police had to face.

To the liberal, a crowd is an aggregate of individuals and consequently of individual rights. But with any gathering the interests of other people, both as individuals and as the 'public', are adversely affected. Competing rights and public interest both provide subtly different justifications for the dispersal of a crowd or the arrest of participants, as opposed to the more formal criteria required for arrest for an individual theft or assault. The practical basis of police judgement rests on how senior officers assess the 'public interest' and the 'balance' of competing rights. That judgement shows very little concern for collective political or industrial rights and more for public 'tranquillity', though, as I shall argue, that word begs many questions and is far from being a straightforward neutral description of social order.

The Use of Force

It is increasingly accepted nowadays that it is justified to confront crowds with force. This poses further threats to any political consensus on collective rights. Violence is not an innovation—a century ago the use of the army and militia was common, protecting the lives and property of the upper and middle classes and the authority of the government. In November 1887 socialist demonstrations in Trafalgar Square were broken up by detachments of the Life Guards and the Foot Guards,[1] but the army have not confronted civilians since the General Strike (although they have carried out various essential tasks, such as firefighting, during industrial disputes since 1945).

In the eighteenth and nineteenth centuries crowds normally directed their anger at property and not at people.[2] Even when crowds attacked the soldiers, it was with stones—often answered by volleys of shots. There was no guarantee that bystanders would not be killed—in the Featherstone shootings in 1893 one victim was James Gibbs, a Sunday School teacher who, the jury said, 'was a peaceful man and took no part in riotous proceeding'. Then in the miners' strikes of 1910 and 1911 there were the fatal shootings of miners in Tonypandy and Llanelli. The army's approach, through its training and organization, was necessarily inflexible, all participants being treated alike. The military 'solution' was often fatal force, out of proportion to the violence of the demonstrators.

From 1910 there was a government policy to avoid employing the military, and it has slowly become accepted that only the police are entitled to use force. One of the last examples of the use of the military was in the 1919 police strike, when troops with fixed bayonets confronted police strikers in Liverpool. Since the First World War crowd control has been the task of the police who, as in no other country, have adopted policies of being unarmed and of using 'minimum force', whether on patrol or in the control of crowds.

Indeed, there was a noticeable decline in violent confrontations from the 1920s until the 1970s. There were exceptions, notably the repression of the marches of the National Unemployed Workers Movement in the 1930s.[3] But Geary's study of the policing of industrial disputes plots the change in the behaviour of crowds from the missile- and stone-throwing of the late nineteenth century to the relatively innocuous 'pushing and shoving' of the 1970s and the decline in the state's violence from firearms to the use of baton charges. Unlike soldiers, constables were trained to operate independently and to enforce the law on their own responsibility. They provided a different and flexible response to the problems of crowd control. The tactics available to the unarmed constable were necessarily limited: the officer must work to defuse situations rather than rely on defensive equipment or firepower. Crowds responded in kind: '[disputes] were characterised by order rather than disorder. On the whole strikers refrained from rioting, destroying property and even the kind of violent picketing that took place before the war. Many of the relatively few violent clashes that did occur were provoked by the police or the Specials.'[4] After the Second World War a certain constitutionalism had evolved over collective rights and around the conduct of political and industrial demonstrations. Violence to people or property was rare, police intervention was by and large minimal, and though the legal rights to march, meet, or picket might be obscure, the right to do so within a political consensus was well established.

Since the mid-1970s this constitutional truce has disappeared—the use of violence by and against crowds is commonplace; the ambiguity of the legal rights has been replaced by clearer and more restrictive policing powers in the Public Order Act 1986. In the past decade, both the behaviour of crowds (back to the brick-throwing and petrol-bombing property damage and looting of the nineteenth century) and the pattern of police responses have totally changed. The mutual-aid provisions under s. 14 of the Police Act, 1964 enabling (but not compelling) Chief Constables to send officers to assist other forces, have been revitalized; Police Support Units (PSUs) now exist within all forces so that a proportion (10 per cent) of any force are trained in crowd-control techniques and, though engaged on normal divisional duties at any time, can form a mobile reserve for public-order duties; the National Reporting Centre under the auspices of ACPO has taken on the task of co-ordinating the police response to major 'disturbances'; specialist public-order groups such as the Metropolitan's Territorial Support Groups exist in a majority of forces and are on permanent standby; the weaponry has become more sophisticated and is as offensive in intent as it is defensive, including the long night stick, the round shield, baton rounds (plastic bullets), CS gas, and water cannon; not only handguns and rifles are available, but also shotguns and sub-machine-guns.

There is a new capacity to mobilize massed ranks of police in opposition to a crowd. At Orgreave on 29 May 1984 there were 1,700 officers from thirteen different forces confronting 1,500 pickets. It was the closure of another coking works by miners, Saltley, in 1972, that led police chiefs to re-evaluate public order strategy. But such tactics increase the risks of violent confrontation. At Orgreave in May and June stones and bottles were thrown and baton charges were made on horseback and by helmeted riot squads. Hundreds were injured so that the works should remain open: one miner with a fractured skull had to have the kiss-of-life.

The constables' role has changed. Acting in concert on commands from senior officers, they are no longer exercising the authority of responsibility of the 'independent office-holder' or using legitimate criteria—that is, the assessment of individuals' liabilities for their actual or potential criminal acts. The police have developed the use of 'snatch squads' to penetrate into the crowd, quickly arrest an alleged 'ringleader', and retreat with their catch behind the lines. But in the main the crowd is treated as a single entity with all participants equally responsible. The violence meted out by police baton charges or through police horses is indiscriminate and the basis of arrests is often arbitrary: subsequent court cases have frequently shown that police evidence is either flimsy or untrue. In 1979, in prosecutions arising out of the Southall disturbances, at least one officer gave evidence under oath of the arrest of one defendant at a particular time and place whereas the previous day he had testified to arresting another suspect in a different place at the same time. The 'crime' appears to be participation in the demonstration.

These developments highlight the vulnerability of collective protest, the lack of entrenched political freedoms, and the limited extent to which individuals can rely on civil liberties. The consensus within which minority protest was tolerated has also been eroded, both by the tactics of mass confrontational policing and by the new public-order legislation. Collective dissent is to be met by legal as well as physical force.

Public Order in Democracy

The justification for these changes is that the overall public interest must be given priority over individual rights or collective political freedoms. Demonstrations are a threat to public order or tranquillity and this is a precondition of personal security. The concept of 'peace' as a civilizing and unifying element has a long tradition—in Anglo-Saxon and Anglo-Norman England, each lord within the feudal hierarchy would have his 'peace' which gave him jurisdiction over specific territory and persons. The king's peace slowly came to be general and to protect the whole country and all subjects. The allegation of a 'breach of the king's peace' enabled the king's court to claim jurisdiction over a wide range of legal and administrative matters and was an important factor in the political centralization of the country in the twelfth and thirteenth centuries. But 'peace' was not an abstraction—the order that it represented protected the property rights of the aristocracy and the social relationships and political authority which rested upon those rights. This was shown by the bitterness with which the expansion of the royal jurisdiction was contested, not least in the barons' confrontation with John which led to the king's recognizing traditional baronial rights through Magna Carta. But by Tudor times the king's peace was supreme—Henry VII and his successors were absolute monarchs and the feudal aristocracy were a protected but subordinate class.

If the negotiation of the 'peace' was part of the political

battleground in the development of the feudal monarchy, an echo of the same theme on social and political authority is found in the modern debate over 'law and order'. 'Law' and 'order' are not synonyms and there can be conflicting ideas as to the 'proper' nature of their combination. On one side it is a legal or liberal democratic concept in which 'law' and individual rights take priority. Order is not simply regularity, pattern, conformity, and tranquillity in everyday life; it is a more complex notion—the knowledge that person and property are protected not by patronage or physical might but by rights is a form of order which signifies the stability and health of social and constitutional arrangements. 'Law' implies an underlying permanence or natural quality which should not be crudely manipulated to benefit sections of society: even the democratic majority needs to respect the interests of the minority.

The alternative perspective reverses this with straightforward elements of 'order' taking precedence over 'law'. 'Order' is based on an acceptance of authority in which personal security is ensured by the State but at a cost of personal freedoms. People are expected to defer to and accept the authority of a government and its agents.

How do the police conceive of 'order'? Their immediate motivations are based on occupational and institutional interests, especially control and especially on the streets. In public, people should be routinely walking, shopping, or passing the time of day. Any crowd in a public space (or indeed in a private hall) constitutes police business. For the tidy housekeepers of the police, crowds are disorderly. They disrupt the routine flow of people and vehicles.

Alongside the grand scale of protest and demonstration is the everyday order of the street. Here police have always sought to prevent crowds forming and have aroused hostility by 'moving on' individuals and small groups. The constable treats public space as private territory, imposing 'order' by saying what can and cannot be done. The ability to do this is a measure of authority, that of the officer both as an individual and that of the police as an institution. Within this microcosm of control a theory of order is implied which depends not on recognition of rights but on deference to authority, 'doing what you're told'. Nor is this a democratic concept of authority—senior officers have at all times shown themselves hostile to direct links between elected political bodies and the police. They emphasize the role of the police as being above the sectional interests of political parties and portray the preservation of the peace and the enforcement of the law as reflecting universal interests for a society. They derive their authority from enforcing a 'public interest' that resides neither in politics, nor in law, nor in entrenched constitutional liberties but in traditional beliefs about power and class.

The clearest examples arise in industrial disputes. Geary[5] quotes Bramshill lecturers who recommend that officers contact management to see whether normal working is to be maintained and deliveries and collections made, to elicit the attitude of the workforce to the dispute and the possibility of providing buses for the employees and identification marks for employees' vehicles. We have already seen that many forces did exactly this during the miners' strike, and by providing buses to transport workers used police resources for a straightforward political objective—to promote a move among NUM members to go back to work. Geary further quotes a Chief Superintendent who had arranged for a different means of distribution for a local newspaper during a journalists' strike. What does not happen is a formal, high-level negotiation with the union to ensure, for instance, that pickets are able to present a case to employees or delivery drivers. On-the-spot compromises are reached to reduce tension but the 'disorder' is by definition that of the workers. It has been the police's task throughout their history to control and segregate, by whatever means they have at their disposal, not merely tramps, drunks, and prostitutes but also unions, radical and not-so-radical political activists, minorities, and inner city populations.

When senior officers fall back on the language of 'order' or 'tranquillity' they are not discussing an abstract state of affairs, removed from the social and political conflict of everyday life. It is language that cannot be politically neutral: 'Whose order?' is a pertinent question. The police definition coincides with a politically conservative model of order[6] that regards existing democratic procedures and institutions as adequate to advance the interests of all groups within society, all of whom are presumed to be equally capable of making their views known and taken into account in a pluralist system of decision-making. To a Conservative, collective action must be seen as an illegitimate distortion of this process as it seeks to manipulate through the 'irrationality' of the mass to achieve objectives that could not be gained through more formal constitutional channels.

The Marxist perspective is sceptical about the 'equal and

consensual' society implied in the conservative model. It sees a society riven by inequalities of power and class conflict concealed by ideological abstractions such as public interest or law and order. These assume consensus but disguise class interests and help to ensure the continuing domination of capital over labour. Inevitably there is collective protest against that domination. Historians have undertaken considerable research into crowds over the past twenty years and at the hands of Hobsbawm, Rudé, Thompson, and Tilly[7] the role of the crowd in history has undergone a reassessment. As 'poor men's politics', riots were the means of expression of the powerless and inarticulate, a proto-democratic institution before the development of constitutional mechanisms for political expression. Modern conflict theorists similarly argue that a riot cannot be written off as degenerate and irrational behaviour. The physical and ideological power of certain economic and political groups means that collective action, even collective aggression, is sometimes necessary to achieve change. It would be mistaken to see the 1960s riots in American cities as 'meaningless violence': they presaged a significant change in racial attitudes in the USA, and indeed the rise of black political power through election to a whole range of public offices in major cities. In Britain, the city disturbances of the 1980s have consistently included protests at the racialism of our society.

Although the liberal view plays down the elements of class and power, it has always recognized the legitimacy of collective expression of interests, especially in industrial or political contexts. This was shown by the battles in previous centuries for the right to meet, march, and demonstrate and for the freedom of speech and thought. Added to this is the central liberal tenet of acceptance of the beliefs and actions of others. Nor is this simply a matter of democratic balance sheets—minority rights are as important as those of the majority. As Dworkin[8] says, 'A right against the Government must be a right to do something even when the majority thinks it would be wrong to do it, and even when the majority would be worse off for having it done.'

Within a liberal society, order has to be more than tranquillity—it is a more deep-seated consensus which accepts challenges to political authority or dislocation of the market place as crucial elements. Through such conflicts the stability of constitutional relationships is shown to rely not on repression of an exploited and powerless class but on the development of a delicate balance, achieved by allowing freedom to individual and collective expression and by recognizing the rights of minorities.

Balancing Rights

It has never been part of the language of the politicians or the police to deny the liberal image of fundamental rights. But, as we have seen, the legitimacy of demonstrations and strikes is constantly attacked. The police often act as if they were 'entitled to regard all the demonstrators as potential rioters and as legitimate targets for pre-emptive strikes'.[9] A traditional justification is in terms of the overall 'public interest' but a more sophisticated argument is that of 'balance'—the right to demonstrate, to march, to meet, even to picket, is accepted but it is counterposed against other rights and duties:

A balance has to be struck, a compromise found that will accommodate the exercise of the right to protest within a framework of public order which enables citizens, who are not protesting, to go about their business and pleasure, without obstruction or inconvenience. The fact that those who are at any one time concerned to secure the tranquillity of the streets are likely to be the majority must not lead us to deny the protestors the right to march: the fact that the protestors are desperately sincere and are exercising a fundamental human right must not lead us to overlook the rights of the majority.

   This Inquiry has been concerned to discover where the balance should be struck and the role of the police in maintaining it.[10]

'Maintaining the balance' is an extraordinarily difficult task when the National Front marches through East London or the Orange Order through a Catholic district of Belfast. Throughout their history the police have held bitterly opposed factions at bay. They now, under the Public Order Act 1986, have a new ground for intervention, 'serious disruption to the life of the community', implying that the police must draw a balance between the rights of the demonstrators and those of the local residents. But the Act does not spell out what constitutes 'disruption': that is left to the police who are able to re-route a march away from the town centre where it would get maximum publicity and instead lead it through the back streets of the town.

   While the theory of 'balance' is admirable, in practice massed police presence on picket lines (and running a taxi service for non-strikers) has been portrayed as balancing the right to strike against the 'right to work'. At Wapping, enabling distribution lorries to leave the News International plant throughout the 1986–7 dispute was 'balancing' Rupert Murdoch's right to run his business against the rights of the sacked print workers. The weight of State machinery on one side of the scale destroys any such theory of 'balance'.

Such examples show the police pursuing objectives which are not policing objectives. The demonstration by Manchester University students against the visit of Home Secretary Leon Brittan in March 1985 is a further illustration. Some hundreds of students were peacefully blocking the steps of their union building to prevent Leon Brittan from entering. It was a symbolic gesture as there was another entrance at the back. When the Home Secretary refused to use this, the police, without warning, attempted to force a path and charged into the crowd, throwing people down the steps and causing dozens of injuries. Was the objective to maintain the Home Secretary's right of passage or his dignity? A Police Complaints Authority report, a summary of which was published two years later, spoke of serious mismanagement of a peaceful demonstration.

In industrial disputes the language of 'balance' is used to undermine the right of collective protest and conceal the political purpose behind a discretionary and highly marginal police use of public resources. Normally the police are unwilling to intervene in matters of civil law, as landlords seeking to evict squatters have discovered. The protection of private rights to enter your place of employment or carry on a business should be through the civil courts, perhaps not even indirectly through the criminal law. News International, for example, obtained an injunction ordering SOGAT and the NGA not to organize mass pickets at the Wapping plant—should the police enforce that injunction? At this point, senior officers can be ordered by the court to intervene, though as we shall see in Chapter 7, in non-industrial situations the courts are reluctant to interfere with the police's operational discretion. In strikes and lockouts it is arguable that courts should simply use the sanctions of money damages and contempt of court, rather than compelling the police to take sides.

We draw distinctions between private law and public law—with the former, the enforcement of contractual and property rights should be seen as a matter for the individuals and the courts and not for the police who are in no position to adjudicate the rights in question. The same is not true of maintaining a balance of rights exercisable in public. These are rights which are common to us all. Order is important so that people can use public space for lawful purposes, but what is too rarely acknowledged is that demonstrators are going about a lawful purpose until there is a breach of the criminal law. The 'majority' has the right to pass and repass along the highway, the shopper and the car driver are 'inconvenienced' by public gatherings, and their rights are important, but the disturbance is a temporary and minor one when placed alongside Scarman's 'fundamental right'. But the police still treat these everyday irritations as directly comparable with a major touchstone of any liberal society, that is, the right to protest: 'The conflict between the right of peaceful protest and that of citizens to go about their lives without roads blocked off, traffic diverted or the inconvenience of noise, places the police in another of society's quandaries.'[11] Such statements reveal the inadequacies of a public-order strategy based on 'balance' and an undifferentiated set of rights, whether private or public. Derogation from fundamental rights is acceptable only when the threatened harm is immediate and serious.

Public Order Strategy

While the conservative would see demonstration as inherently illegitimate and the Marxist as one of the tactics of the class struggle, liberal policy would protect the legitimacy of collective expression. These different attitudes to social order and the role of crowds imply different public-order strategies. For the conservative, public marches or meetings should not be used to challenge authority; the police should have the means to reassert that authority and the demonstrator is voluntarily abandoning the protective shield of civil rights. This is in many ways a description of the new tactics of crowd-control and the libertarian would take issue on all of these, especially on the development of para-military means. But is this simply reflex criticism?

There is an important issue here which critics of the police have not reflected on enough. In violent confrontations, a 'non-militaristic' response by police (i.e. one where they do not have adequate training, manpower, co-ordination and defensive and even offensive equipment) may mean that injuries will be multiplied. . . If the use of violence by the police is necessary, it must be handled efficiently rather than aggravated by incompetence or default. The very hard issue of how to cope with collective disorder is simply dodged by the critics . . . the thrust of much critical comment seems to deny legitimacy to *any* public order strategy . . .[12]

When the focus of attention is the courage of constables in the face of missiles hurled by marauding Millwall supporters or petrol bombs at Broadwater Farm, then it is easy to concentrate on the mechanics of how the police are best able to restore immediate order. The issue is made more complex when the focus shifts to encompass the aggression of the police themselves, the contribution that policing policies have made to the riots, or the displacement of policing objectives by political ones.

Before proposing contemporary strategies on the 'how' of crowd control, it may be useful to provide a historical perspective. 'Riots' were more common in the past than they are today, but their targets were almost invariably property and not people. Rudé's study of English riots from the 1730s to the 1840s produces 'remarkably few fatal casualties among the rioters' victims'. Rudé can find only a handful of examples but comments: 'This record contrasts sharply with the toll of life exacted among the rioters by the military and the law courts', and cites the twenty-five Gordon rioters and the thirty Luddites hanged, or the 100 colliers killed or wounded at Hexham in 1761.[13] The conclusion that the military or the police were used as a disciplinary mechanism still has relevance in the twentieth century. On hearing of the settlement of a railway strike in 1911, Churchill is said to have telephoned Lloyd George and told him: 'I'm very sorry to hear it. It would have been better to have gone on and given these men a good thrashing.' In June 1985 the police quite brutally attacked a convoy of hippies travelling to Stonehenge. In 1986 the Earl of Cardigan, the owner of Savernake Forest where the attack took place, wrote to the *Guardian*: 'the police suggested to me on the Sunday morning, 12 hours after the battle, that I agree to them sending in "some hundreds" of riot police to the camp site which was full of women and children, "to finish unfinished business".'

Reiner's concern is with the method of coping with collective disorder. Yet if we examine the new strategies of mass policing and the weaponry of 'riot' control, the implications are not managerial but relate to the coercive imposition of political authority. This is recognized by a Chief Superintendent quoted by Geary:[14] 'once the mind has achieved another diameter of thought it doesn't return to its original size. We've got all this stuff and it may well be that you can put a helmet on, pick up a truncheon and shield, pull your visor down and achieve more with one man than you did before with three. It's very tempting.'

The development of such a strategy seems disastrous on several fronts. First, it has undermined many of the constructive moves towards community policing which have occurred not just in the inner cities but also, for instance, in mining communities. Secondly, not only the practical legacy of bitterness after such operations but also the blatant rejection of many of the principles of fairness (neutrality, accountability, the minimum use of force) erode public confidence in the police. Thirdly, the para-military and pre-emptive nature of these operations is needlessly provocative and has led to an escalation of violence.

Ideally, perhaps idealistically, the elements of a public-order strategy should be dramatically different. *Neutrality* is clearly essential in industrial or political situations—the police must be seen to be non-aligned and leave the issues to be dealt with by legal or political processes. As part of this there must be a recognition that collective protest not only is legitimate but is one of the most important practical symbols of a liberal society—to that end any police force should be *facilitative*. In 1987 negotiations between police and hippies led to access to Stonehenge and an orderly summer solstice, in marked contrast to the previous year. (Exactly the opposite occurred in Red Lion Square when the police used the actions of a few as justification for the violent dispersal of some 1,500 peaceful demonstrators. And at Wapping, pickets were given no opportunity to explain the nature of the dispute to lorry drivers who entered and left the printing plant at speed. At least one death resulted from this policy when a lorry knocked down a picket. No prosecution followed.) The ideal approach would be based on the ethos of constitutional policing generally—that it should be *reactive*, intervening only where serious offences have taken place and using the broad public-order powers only where necessity dictates. These are policing targets—other problems should be left to the courts or the government.

This strategy would rely on fewer officers for crowd control, using normal equipment. It would depend on the courts, on collective bargaining procedures, or on political processes to resolve the matters in dispute or to support government authority. There are limits to the usefulness of the criminal law and its enforcement agencies. In the words of Hartley Shawcross,[15] Attorney-General in the post-war Labour government: 'You might as well try to bring down a rocket bomb with a peashooter as to try to stop a strike by the process of the criminal law. The way to stop strikes is not by a policeman but by a conciliation officer, not by the assize courts but by arbitration tribunals.'

But in the aftermath of the inner-city disturbances of 1981 and 1985, the constant battles at football grounds on Saturday afternoons, or the potential for violent clashes when two opposing factions stage counter-demonstrations, such a prescription must seem disingenuous. Naturally where violence occurs, Reiner's strictures apply on the need for a professional and effective response to limit the damage. But the demands for police with riot-training are rare, whereas the need for sensible and consensual policing of strikes and marches is constantly with us. In such everyday situations, the mass police presence is already the norm, with the potential consequences suggested earlier. The answer is not to develop a third force between police and army, a riot police along the lines of the cynical and brutal French CRS. Only too quickly such a force assumes total responsibility for public order, with a consequent decline in standards. Maintaining public order has traditionally been part of the general duties of the police and should continue to be. There is a need for selective training of adequate numbers of officers in crowd-control techniques, and for defensive equipment. Yet it is the management of crowds—when, where, and how to act—that is the core issue. Should it be left to the police to make these decisions, or should they be accountable to some democratic process?

6

Policing Private Lives

The Public and the Private

We live in an era when we are forced to disgorge information about ourselves for the benefit of the tax, health, education, let alone police, authorities. They all possess considerable powers over people's lives. In the last chapter it was argued that there was a dichotomy between the public and the private, between the regulated public world and the unregulated private life. Thus the policing of the public is generally regarded as legitimate, but how far are we entitled to a sphere of privacy, immune from interference by the police?

The private may be considered as that domain of thoughts, beliefs, and behaviour which is unregulated by the State. But are there criteria which mark a definitive boundary? Even liberal and democratic states intervene into religious or political belief, economic transactions, or biological and social reproduction. The market may be 'free' but there is legislation on trades descriptions and unfair contract terms to protect the consumer. Forms of sexual behaviour are criminalized; family size is indirectly regulated through child-benefit levels. The language of privacy provides no obvious boundaries.

We speak of privacy but whether we are looking at the family or the school, the workplace or the home, state intervention is often fundamental in shaping social attitudes and beliefs as well as in influencing behaviour. Is the dichotomy between the private and the public simply false? Feminists such as O'Donovan[1] argue that ideas of 'privacy' are used to preclude certain forms of intervention in the family but that this rhetoric masks and reinforces the inequalities of power within the politics of the family: 'In feminist translation, the private is a sphere of battery, marital rape and women's exploited labour; of the central social institutions whereby women are deprived of (as men are granted) identity, autonomy, control and self-determination.' She goes on to argue that a lack of direct involvement does not mean a lack of state policy—the vacuum merely cedes power and authority within the family to the male. This supports patriarchy as much as any more intrusive stance by the State would do. For many writers on the family, the language of 'the private' is an ideological device which justifies non-intervention and thereby underpins patriarchal dominance. In the economic sphere many materialists also see the language of privacy as ideology, so that the immunity of the market from detailed regulation is able to protect the interests of capital over labour in a *laissez-faire* climate.

But is it premature to reject 'privacy' as having neither analytical nor political value? Can we define a realm of 'private life' that is the business neither of the State nor of the police? Privacy has been an important element in the protection of civil liberties, used by religious and political dissenters to censor state action and maintain a sphere of freedom of action by restraining the powers of the State *vis-à-vis* the individual. Many countries expressly protect rights of privacy in their constitutions (although this in itself would not make privacy any less of an ideological cloak). However, I will argue that there is a concrete quality about the concept of privacy—not least in the language of everyday life which takes for granted personal, internal worlds. Our relationships with others rest on the recognition of those, and of our own private identity. Though difficult to define and often abused, the domain of the private has social meanings the maintenance of which is important for any society, however organized. But, in our formally liberal world, how far has the edifice already been eroded?

Special Branch and Police Surveillance

The police have always gathered and stored information about individuals—criminal records were an early development. Special Branch originated in 1883 as the Special Irish Branch to deal with the Fenian bombing campaign and by the 1960s comprised some 300 officers mainly centred in London. By the early 1980s the number had increased to at least 400 officers based in London, with a further 1,250 around the country.

The objects of Special Branch surveillance were spelt out by Home

Secretary Merlyn Rees in 1978: 'The Special Branch collects information on those who I think cause problems for the State.' The duties include guarding Royalty and other VIPs, watching ports and airports, liaising with MI5, monitoring the Irish and other alien communities, following up offences under the Official Secrets Acts, and seeing to the conduct of elections. But Special Branch also garner information on activities which they see as subversive or potentially subversive—in the 1930s they infiltrated the National Unemployed Workers Movement and collected lists of names of all those who volunteered to fight in the Spanish Civil War. Nowadays unions, left-wing groups, CND, and Greenpeace among others would be routinely scrutinized. Demonstrators and pickets will find themselves photographed. Even minor local meetings will be the object of surveillance—the local police are under a duty to inform Special Branch of all known political and industrial meetings. If Special Branch do not attend, then the local CID must complete a form detailing names of speakers and organizers. This extends to legitimate and innocuous gatherings—in 1979 Greenwich Women's Voice were approached by the local officer for help in filling out the form!

The means of gathering information are not always so naïve—Manwaring-White[2] has surveyed the techniques of spying on the population, not merely by Special Branch but by other security agencies and by the regular forces. Technological advance has made monitoring of telephone conversations relatively easy: a centre in Ebury Bridge Road, London, is capable of monitoring 1,000 calls at any time, and this is not the only listening post. It is a capacity far in excess of any need revealed by the published statistics on authorized tapping. Video cameras have become commonplace at football matches where they are often a valuable and legitimate tactic: in January 1987 they were responsible for arrests of Millwall and West Ham followers, and video recordings played a major part in the investigation following the Heysel Stadium tragedy in Brussels in 1985. But there are also video cameras scanning strategic points in London, such as the one on top of the National Gallery, overlooking Trafalgar Square. They are formally designated as traffic control cameras, but outside the American Embassy in Grosvenor Square, they are also useful for monitoring political demonstrations.

Somewhat sinister is the camera placed at the north exit to the
Dartford Tunnel, able to scan the number plates of cars and directly
linked to a data base containing lists of stolen cars. As Manwaring-
White points out, such a system can be programmed for other
purposes—the Police National Computer (PNC) holds a list not
merely of stolen vehicles but of ones which are regarded as suspicious
or of long-term interest for some reason other than the commission of
crime. In 1981 the political editor of the *New Statesman*, Peter
Kellner, found that his new car was included on the list—was it
accident, or because of his left-wing affiliations, or because of a recent
holiday in Ireland?

Night vision equipment, fibre optics, and a wide range of bugging
devices are all available. Helicopters with long-range cameras can be
used to monitor all manner of gatherings and in the US they have
been used to spray crowds with CS gas. In Northern Ireland helicopters are ubiquitous, not so much for the purposes of countering crime
and gathering information but to harass and intimidate, even at IRA
funerals.

Alongside the developing means of gathering information there are
efficient means of storage in and retrieval from computerized data-
bases. Old-fashioned card-indexes were a substantial protection for
the individual as their very inefficiency militated against the gathering or storing of anything but essential information. Computers
give the potential of infinitely large and infinitely retrievable
data bases. Twenty years ago the local policeman held some of that
information in his head, but now centralization and immediate availability removes it from that context and effectively changes the
quality of surveillance—it is no longer a human process, flexible and
tolerant.

Computerization can be presented as mere managerial pragmat-
ism, whereby some non-controversial administrative function is
carried out more efficiently. But even were it subject to stringent
safeguards, it possesses a capacity for minute regulation of the individual life that demands a reassessment of underlying constitutional
principles—are we ever willing to concede that degree of control to
the State?

The development of computerized police data-bases dates from
1973 when the PNC was established at Hendon with the capacity to
hold 40 million records. It is now linked by VDU to every police

station. By radio link, every beat constable has immediate access to PNC records which include:

(*a*) 120,000 records on a stolen/suspect vehicles file (only a quarter of these are actually stolen);

(*b*) 19 million records transferred from the Driver and Vehicle Licensing Computer (DVLC) located at Swansea;

(*c*) 3.8 million names on the Criminal Names Index which has a capacity of 5.7 million;

(*d*) an index to the 3.25 million fingerprints held in the National Fingerprint Unit;

(*e*) 50,000 names on the wanted/missing persons list; and

(*f*) 170,000 names on the disqualified drivers list.

The Metropolitan force has its own computer system, on-line in 1977 with half of its capacity devoted to Special Branch files. A total of 1.15 million nominal files are maintained by Special Branch, with 300,000 major individual files which are added to at the rate of 2,000 per month. The rest of the computer's capacity is used for intelligence for fraud, serious crimes, drugs, and immigration intelligence. Much of the data on the computer is hard information, but there is also a substantial proportion of unsubstantiated hearsay and speculation.

Provincial forces also maintain their own systems—several, such as Dorset, have developed valuable and effective computerized 'Command and Control' systems, recording reported incidents, maintaining a log of available vehicles and personnel, and dispatching them to the incident. The Metropolitan force has recently introduced the most ambitious of such systems.

More controversially, Thames Valley have experimented with computerizing the collator—that is, the officer who collates reports and incidents from various sources and seeks to draw out the implications for crime control. For nearly ten years at Thames Valley's headquarters in Kidlington, a computer has recorded and collated information about individuals, even though they may be quite innocent of any criminal involvement and the information recorded might be inaccurate gossip.

Private organizations such as the right-wing Economic League allegedly receive police information on the criminal records, bank accounts, and car numbers as part of their service of vetting employees for some 2,000 leading British companies. It holds files on some 250,000 people whom it regards as politically subversive, including CND members, Friends of the Earth, and animal rights and anti-apartheid campaigners.

The general value of computerized information banks or management systems is undoubted. But their use in crime control is a different matter. Computers may have uses in pinpointing a specific *modus operandi*, investigating the personal characteristics of a suspect, or in some individual investigations storing and handling the vast amount of information gleaned from painstaking house-to-house enquiries. However, the criticisms start at the point at which 'intelligence' diverges from 'information'—people not convicted of a crime can find themselves on file; much of the information is low-level and inaccurate; there is a lack of security enabling non-police agencies such as banks or credit organizations to gain access; there is no protection or redress against abuse since the Data Protection Act specifically exempts police files from outside scrutiny.

The general justification for all these surveillance techniques with their expensive equipment is 'crime prevention': they are said to be necessary both to combat the increasing sophistication of organized crime and of groups that use mass violence for political ends, and to deal with crowd disorder. This is a valid rationale for a targeted and limited approach, for instance video surveillance of a football ground with a past history and present threat of violence would be justified in terms of both detection and deterrence. But the immediate objective of monitoring a political demonstration or a picket is to gather information and intelligence, not usually on immediate and direct threats but for indirect and speculative purposes. It was argued in Chapter 3 that the police have only a limited ability to alter crime rates in general and that enhanced technical capacity is unlikely to change that. That technical capacity is aimed not specifically at 'criminals' or 'terrorists' but at the population at large.

Computerized data-banks encourage this surveillance. The overall strategy of the former Metropolitan Commissioner, Newman, was to employ targeting and surveillance techniques to identify potential police problems: 'I believe crime intelligence to be essential to the Metropolitan police and I consider the continued development of an integrated crime intelligence system to be of strategic importance to the force.'[3] This 'integrated' system (the Crime Reports Information System) relies on low-level intelligence garnered by local beat officers or supplied through Neighbourhood Watch schemes, with no guarantee that it is founded on anything more than suspicion or prejudice. The justification, somewhat disingenuous, is simply that the honest citizen has nothing to fear. But in West Germany a change of government led to a systematic sacking of all teachers and other government employees listed as having Communist affiliations.

Yet the practical dangers of such records to the individual are not the real issue—the problem is not a pragmatic but a moral and constitutional one. A critical aspect of your individuality is the monopoly of private knowledge about yourself that you alone possess or might share with a cherished other person. The acquisition of 'knowledge' about other individuals is often used as a source of power over them. In Orwell's *1984*, Winston Smith's interrogator O'Brien rehearses aspects of Winston's life ('For seven years I have watched over you . . . I shall save you, I shall make you perfect') to establish psychological command: 'Then the time has come for you to take the last step. You must love Big Brother. It is not enough for you to obey him: you must love him.'

Liberalism insists on the pivotal position of the individual's privacy—in criminal justice there is a legal 'right to silence' within the police station or the court. Such a rule was formulated when there was limited public knowledge about an individual. The expansion of public records and the state's capacity to scrutinize private lives has occurred without any concomitant safeguards and has rendered the 'right to silence' a near-irrelevancy. A 'right to privacy' should require that individuals are protected from the arbitrary gathering and storing of information about their lives except under specified conditions, one of which should be the threatened or actual committing of a crime. Currently any 'right to privacy' is simply at the discretion of some functionary within the machinery of the state.

Of course, Special Branch monitor political and industrial groups rather than the individual, but the same principle should apply— actions should remain free from state intervention or surveillance unless a crime (or a substantial threat of one) has occurred. Instead, policing helps to delineate the boundaries of 'acceptable' political activity, which is seen as activity within mainline political groupings acting through the ballot box and is protected by concepts of privacy. But even here, ex-MI5 agent Peter Wright has documented scrutiny by the security agencies of Labour politicians, even of ministers. To be part of an 'extra-parliamentary' opposition, ecological, anti-nuclear, nationalist, or Communist, is to invite considerable police interest, even when action is limited to legitimate forms of political and industrial protest. The 'good citizen', though politically concerned, is in essence passive.

Neighbourhood Watch

In *1984* George Orwell's hero is constantly watched by a neighbour's child for signs of deviance ('You're a traitor!' yelled the boy. 'You're a thought criminal'). Orwell's predicted date was a year late. On 6 September 1983, the Metropolitan Police launched Neighbourhood Watch along the lines of 'blockwatchers' schemes in the US. This project is designed to get local residents to co-operate with the police to 'protect themselves and their community from burglars and thieves'. The residents are encouraged to act as 'eyes and ears' and to inform the police of suspicious characters; to mark property so that it can be easily identified; and to improve home security through offering sensible crime prevention. Each scheme was to involve a maximum of some 500 households with a local co-ordinator liaising with a special constable or the local beat officer. This was rapidly followed by other forces and in June 1987 there were 29,000 schemes, also known as Crime Watch or Home Watch, nationwide.

This echoes the tradition of the police as a service industry, directly linked with and responding to the needs of local communities. This is very sensible in the light of the earlier argument that the public, not the police, are largely the discoverers and solvers of crime. The objectives of the scheme include reducing anxiety about crime, especially for the old, taking sensible precautions, and encouraging a co-operative spirit between neighbours. This is reflected in the language used by the police in fostering the project: partnership, social contract, corporate strategy, community, consent. The Neighbourhood Watch initiative links in with Newman's thoughts on 'multi-agency' policing. Donnison[4] has defined this as the coordination by the police of various central government departments such as the DHSS, local authority departments such as education, social services, and housing, as well as voluntary organizations. 'Officers should be seen to be the front-runners in social change whether it is urging architectural change to help in the "designing out" of crime, advocating alternative housing policies or actively persuading commercial enterprises to build greater safety or crime prevention factors into house or vehicle design.'[5]

The strategy developed by the police over the past fifteen years has been a bifurcated one. The multi-agency/Neighbourhood Watch is 'soft' policing, characterized by the home-beat officer, community-liaison officers, or juvenile bureaux. The stress is on consultation and negotiation with the community. But at the same time the major increase in resources has gone into public-order policing, both in equipment and in training. This represents the confrontational 'hard' aspect of modern policing.

These divergent approaches are in many ways directed at different sectors of the population—Neighbourhood Watch schemes are to be found in those areas already supportive of the police, characterized by a high proportion of owner-occupiers, and where the 'criminals' are perceived as outsiders. They are less likely to be found in areas of public or private tenancies where there is hostility to the police and offences may well be committed by local youths. The police themselves divide the population into the respectable and the disreputable and react differently to those perceived as 'police problems'. But the split in overall strategy, as well as the fact that few resources are allocated to the 'soft' end, might suggest that the 'community' policing initiatives will remain a low priority, distracting attention from the major transformation of the police into an armed, trained, public-order force.

The language of 'partnership', 'social contract', and 'community consent' is not intended to presage any reform that would give communities a substantial say in the policing of a neighbourhood, involving a two-way flow of information, with the police being accountable to the local people as well as the other way round. Neighbourhood Watch schemes have a dominant police role and this is reflected in the multi-agency approach—'crime' is identified as the central problem, the solution to which is a police task with contributions from other agencies. Within a genuinely comprehensive project towards safer neighbourhoods, crime and anti-social behaviour would be one of many interrelated issues. As Donnison says, such an approach takes crime and the fear of crime out of the law-and-order context and places them in a category for community action.

The ideals behind Neighbourhood Watch, though excellent in

theory, need to be protected from abuse. They do not represent the main line of development for modern policing, nor are they allowed to interfere with the institutional needs of the police. Neighbourhood Watch, while promoting crime control, also ensures a one-way flow of intelligence and suspicions from local residents (the eyes and ears of the police) to be collated and stored by the police. It forms part of Newman's 'integrated crime intelligence system' which is of 'strategic importance to the force'. To what extent was this a central objective when these projects were created? What strategy is of importance to the police that entails gathering more intelligence on the civil population, regardless of involvement in crime?

Policing in Schools

The co-operation between police and schools is an example of the Newman multi-agency strategy. It pre-dates Newman—in 1978 a joint circular from the DHSS, the DES, and the Home Office, entitled 'Juveniles: Co-operation between the Police and Other Agencies', urged regular meetings at local level between social services, education officers, and the police. In 1980 the Home Office issued its own Circular to encourage such co-operation. The examples it gave included a North Wales headmaster who formed a dinner club to discuss the problems of particular pupils, Surrey secondary schools which created multi-disciplinary 'care committees' for the same purpose, and the Cheshire police who enlisted the head-teachers' help in identifying truants who were then visited at home by the police Juvenile Department. These are classic illustrations of 'targeting' those who *might* become 'police problems', with other agencies providing a one-way flow of information. The initiatives come from the police and the Home Office whose institutional interests and values predominate. This stems from the power to take criminal proceedings but also from the 'law-and-order'/'crime-and-punishment' paradigm which overrides any welfare approach which would see anti-social behaviour as just one factor amongst many.

Targeting goes hand-in-hand with gathering information on less formal levels. The School Inspectors' Report for 1983 encourages the growth of informal contacts between police and teachers, with the local beat officer or juvenile liaison officer dropping in at schools for relaxed discussions. As noted in the Advisory Committee on Policing in Schools, the clear purpose is that teachers should talk freely about their pupils. Within the classroom information about parents and children is readily gleaned and staff regularly discuss (not to say gossip about) their charges. Yet only *in extremis* should this stray outside the school walls. If a child confides in a teacher about a parent's drug problem, there is a moral dilemma for the teacher: do the best interests of the child require the social services to be notified? But the dilemma must be confined to the problem of the child's welfare. The machinery which informally encourages the transmission of such information to the police attacks the relationship of trust which should exist between school and pupil, enrolls the teacher as an auxiliary constable.

It is important to maintain the distinction between policing and social work: police training is oriented towards crime and punishment, not towards welfare. The professional–client relationship, with its ethic of confidentiality, does not exist: the constable's relationship to senior officers and the state is intrinsically different from that of the social worker or teacher. The constable is in a chain of command and operates under express orders. In an occupational hierarchy the police officer has different allegiances which are not necessarily to the local community. The social worker, though under occupational constraints, identifies more closely with the interests and welfare of the individual. Although teacher and social worker invade the privacy of pupil or client, the invasion is not so threatening as that of the police.

An intelligence-gathering function is also present in some classroom discussions taken by police officers where children are invited to 'pick up a phone' to inform (anonymously, if necessary) on a fellow pupil. This targeting and intelligence-gathering is linked to crime prevention, but where this is not related to the committing of a crime it breaches the right to personal privacy. Encouraging teachers or schoolchildren to give information casts into doubt the element of trust that is at the root of a school community.

There are other aspects of the police involvement in schools. Traditionally the constable teaches road safety and cycling skills. Now the talks, accompanied by films or slides, are often about police work or the dangers of drugs or talking to strangers. As with other specialist areas, bringing the professional into the school is a worthwhile teaching technique, imparting factual information and stimulating discussion, even if the officer's teaching ability and the teacher's contribution are variable factors.

These visits, however, raise different issues from those of other professionals. First, discussion of crime raises difficult problems of social and moral values which officers are not qualified to teach. Yet their own values will inevitably surface, backed by the authority of the uniform. The ACPS Report suggests that constables inevitably focus on crime as a product of lower-income groups, of separated families, or of drug use, and suggest that answers are to be found in stricter laws, harsher sentences, and more prisons. In the HMI Report for 1983 it was noted that many teachers found the police material 'crude and propagandist in its nature'.

Secondly, the police's overt objective is to win the 'hearts and minds' of children and gain 'their confidence and respect from an early age'. The acceptance by children of the legitimacy of police authority is a key goal—one of particular importance in inner-city schools, where there is a significant proportion of non-white children who are likely to have hostile encounters with the police outside the school. The HMI Report in 1983 was again sceptical about such a role for the police in schools: 'schools cannot be in the business of promoting an unquestioning acceptance of authority however exercised.'

In London these problems were highlighted in 1987 by the banning by some teachers (the Inner London Teachers Association) of any co-operation with the police. This included blacking the 'Have Fun, Take Care' video produced by the Metropolitan Police and warning children of the danger of sex attacks. The teachers were quoted: 'The police motives are anti-black and anti-working class. They want to get into our classrooms to clock the likely lads so that they can pass their names to the juvenile bureau and the collators at their local stations.'[6] But despite these suspicions schools will be forced in this direction, for under the Education Act 1987 head-teachers and governors are under a duty to 'have regard to any such representations which are made to them by the chief officer of police and which are connected with his responsibilities'. Additional money is available for pilot projects on 'social responsibility', which envisage more police presence in the classroom, and the Conservative administration also intends that governors' annual reports shall specifically say what they have done to strengthen school links with the police.

Domestic Missionaries?

Respect for the police officer in any encounter is a significant factor in avoiding arrest. 'Contempt of cop' will often lead to escalation and possible prosecution, especially if there is an interested audience to see how the constable deals with the situation. The imposition of police authority has been noted by historians such as Storch[7] who saw the early police as 'domestic missionaries'—if the nineteenth-century factory imposed an economic discipline on the working class, the police were the moral disciplinarians, replacing the influence of the squire and the Church on the leisure activities of the lower classes.

To what extent do the police represent, and impose, ideals of 'normal' conduct? They play a part in the transmission of values, partly as they are imbedded in their own occupational culture. The typical recruit to the force will be from the skilled working class, above average in the age of leaving the educational system but below average in formal educational qualifications. However, recent years have seen a dramatic rise in new recruits with two A-levels (from 6.7 per cent for men and 10.5 per cent for women in 1974 to 16.7 and 19.5 per cent respectively in 1984) and in graduate entry (in 1984, 13.2 per cent of male recruits and 20.3 per cent of female recruits were graduates). The new recruit is predominantly white, with a small percentage (less than 2 per cent) from ethnic minorities. Many recruits will have seen military service—in 1986 the West Midlands force sent a recruiting team to British army bases in West Germany. Recruits tend to be conventional and conservative, with a higher proportion reading the *Express* or the *Telegraph* than in the population as a whole. A study in 1977[8] suggested that 80 per cent voted Conservative, with the remainder split between the Alliance and Labour, and that 80 per cent voted in all recent elections.

Basic training is still preponderantly learning law and procedure as well as more physical skills, but there is no longer just the 'occasional hour' on the sociology or psychology of crime or 'social' issues. More emphasis is placed on role-playing, on confronting not merely street problems but also prejudices and stereotypical attitudes, especially towards ethnic minorities. But how far have police views changed? 'All a cop can swing in a milieu of marijuana smokers, inter-racial dates and homosexuals is a night stick' was a comment on the American police in the 1960s. In the 1980s, as the Policy Studies Institute study on the Metropolitan police showed, the sheer racialism of police language is appalling,[9] and this intolerance is extended to all unconventional attitudes and behaviour. The 'liberalizing' effects of basic training (only ten weeks in some forces) do not permeate on to the street. Occupational solidarity not only reinforces illiberal attitudes but also weakens inhibitions against the use of violence.

Training can affect police attitudes—over the last few years the police have been bombarded with criticism, from the women's movement and the media, over their treatment of victims of sex offences and battered wives. Representatives of rape crisis centres and women's refuges have increasingly been teaching the police about the reality of women's lives and have noted a marked change of attitude and, more importantly, of operating procedures. Would a similar onslaught on police racialism have similar effects?

It is, however, the middle management of the police, those on Inspectors' Development Courses and the like, who are the beneficiaries of these training initiatives. This stratum of the police hierarchy is increasingly being occupied by graduates, which in theory will lead to more liberal and tolerant attitudes permeating down to patrolling officers as well as a greater willingness to take disciplinary action against racialism. But a gap is likely to open up between the more sophisticated approach of management and the 'macho' culture of the beat officers.

Attitudes inevitably affect everyday policing—the constable's own beliefs affect who may be watched, stopped, or questioned. There is a link between surveillance and judgement—although we may not reassess our own moral character as a result of police scrutiny, the community is more likely to do so. The tritest example is the sight of a patrol car outside a house, which often will excite not merely speculation but disapproval. By their very intervention, the police portray an activity or a person as in some way deviant or abnormal. To be the object of police attention is to invite judgement and this in turn provokes pressure, both internal and external, towards normalized conduct—that is, behaviour conforming to some broad social and cultural values.

The link between police scrutiny and community judgement is strengthened by the British public's deep-seated approval of the police in comparison to other professions. Police attitudes towards activities or persons carry considerable weight. Information on crime and public order is easily and directly obtainable from police press offices and there is little counter-information. The newspaper reader or television watcher rarely has first-hand experience to set against this version. Only with organized labour and industrial disputes or political demonstrations are the police faced with an informed and effective mechanism for disseminating alternative accounts.

The police contribute to public attitudes, not merely to the 'facts' but more broadly towards what is 'normal' conduct. In January 1987 the police not only raided the Vauxhall Tavern, a gay pub, in London, but they did so wearing rubber gloves. Their attitudes maintain that sense of the disreputable, reinforce the image of the deviant, and strengthen particular social beliefs as to how people should live their lives. The gay bookshop, club, or bar will be raided, black youths stopped on the streets, the socialist newspaper-seller moved on. The middle-class driver with children in the back will be cautioned whereas the youth in the old banger will be searched (along with the car) and probably end up in court. The police are part of that social process by which the private personality is scrutinized, judged, and, if possible, normalized.

To the police the 'good' family is the epitome of the normal—the male as wage-earning patriarch and the female as a 'good wife and mother'. They display open disapproval of the single parent or separated wife. Their reluctance to prosecute husbands who assault their wives and failure to co-operate with battered-wives centres displays collusion with the male world—although at the top there is a greater willingness to combat the mentality that classifies domestic violence as 'rubbish'.

The Police and Women

The police have also reassessed their treatment of rape victims—new London centres stress sympathy and support for the woman as opposed to the long and humiliating interrogations which until recently were the norm. As one police inspector wrote in the *Police Review* in 1975, 'it is always advisable if there is any doubt of the truthfulness of the allegations to call her an outright liar'. In 1982, in the BBC documentary *Police*, DC Kirk of Thames Valley confirmed that this approach still held good when he commented on the complainant's story, 'That is the biggest load of bollocks I've ever heard.'

Police investigation procedures still discourage women from reporting rape incidents: in 1982 a 17-year-old hitch-hiking home from a
party was raped by a Suffolk businessman (who was fined £2,000). She
was interviewed, initially in a hostile and disbelieving fashion, for
fourteen hours in three different police stations before being allowed
home. It is still not an atypical story—despite the education of the
public and the police by women's groups, it is not surprising that
rape is the most under-reported of all serious offences of violence.

The threat of male violence is a very real one for women, made so
not merely by the incidence of rape and sexual murder but also by the
pervasive use made of women's bodies by advertising, books, and
newspapers as well as by the constant sexual innuendo and harassment of everyday life. It underpins the power relationships between
men and women which, along with low pay, worse education, and
fewer job opportunities, have traditionally consigned women to the
private and domestic sphere. The public is male territory, characterized by sexual aggression (often perceived as natural and inevitable), and male authority rests on maintaining such a separation.
The police, while on the one hand being the 'protectors', on the other
reinforce the image of the subordinate woman by projecting certain
stereotypical myths about rape and its victims.

The underlying theme is the contrasting sexuality of men and
women—the active, natural, and inevitable aggression of the male
ranged against the passivity of the female, who requires the protection
and patronage of the male. A second image is that rape is not merely a
variant of male sexual aggression but is qualitatively different—the
'genuine' rape is by the 'animal' stranger on a 'respectable' woman. A
rape investigation is divided into two parts—first, the denial that rape
has taken place (it must have been with consent or at least provoked)
and second, the breaking of any link with everyday, 'normal', male
sexual aggression. The 'white-collar' rape by the employer or university lecturer, if ever reported, would often be regarded as 'victim-
precipitated'. Also excluded from the definition would be assaults on
certain statuses of victim such as prostitutes or women dressing in
ways seen as 'provocative' to the 'red-blooded' male—the victim in
the Suffolk case was challenged about her skin-tight jeans. Women
walking alone in public spaces are also jettisoning their right to
protection—hitch-hiking is seen by police and judges as a positive
invitation to sexual attack.

The rape laws have a surface stringency with high maximum penalties. Underneath, their enforcement is lax—Jeffreys and Radford[10] have commented that pro-active policing gives males in public lavatories better protection against sexual assault than it does to women. Further, they argue that women's inability to rely on protection from physical assault is a recurring symbol of male hegemony. Through their policies and procedures the police reinforce the social ideal of the female role—passive, domestic, servicing, and subordinate to the male. Although justifications can be advanced for the police treatment of the rape victim, the underlying message for the victim is a clear one—reinforcing myths about male and female sexuality and underlining the power relationship between men and women, the law leaps to the protection of the woman who is playing her role correctly, chaste or married, properly attired, and suitably dependent on a male. The oddest element in rape is that it is the victim whose life is microscopically examined and judged in the police station and courtroom. It is her success or failure in living up to male myths of femininity which will be judged.

Control of the Streets

Other groups, such as alcoholics, homeless vagrants, ethnic minorities, homosexuals, or left-wing political activists, are also brought within the criminal justice net, but as offenders. Because of their private lives, they are always able, in the last resort, to be defined and processed as 'criminals'. One technique of control is that of social sanitation: the unconventional are made invisible by diversion into institutions (prisons, hospitals, detoxification centres) or into ghettos where the homeless congregate, the prostitutes ply for trade, or a particular ethnic group live. But the visibility of such people is also important—their routine harassment and trial is a modern morality play, signifying social disapproval for those who fail to embrace conventional forms of living. The constant scrutiny and regulation of the lives of gays, drug addicts, and political radicals is not for the defendant but for a wider social audience.

These people are denied the rights of citizenship and privacy that go with liberal society. Those rights are contingent on conformity. The tramp may be beaten up, the prostitute raped, the alcoholic may die on his own vomit—in practice they can lay little claim to police protection since they exist outside of the margins of the respectable. Terming such people 'police property', Reiner comments: 'The prime function of the police has always been to control and segregate such groups.'

The intense police regulation of ethnic communities illustrates this theme: they may be segregated into ghettos; the young urban black may be typecast as the stereotype of the street criminal; they are denied fundamental rights of justice, as evidenced by the continuing failure of the police to counter the threat of racialist attacks in East London. A parallel can be drawn with the position of women—the differential relationships of power between woman and man in a male-dominated society are equivalent to those between black and white in a white world. While feminists would argue that the threat and reality of male violence to women maintain those inequalities, for black communities that violence is embodied in the endemic racialism of the modern police force.

Control of the streets involves the police in the role of moral disciplinarians of society, reinforcing the values of family and market-place which are central to a dominant social and economic class. At a time of decline for established religion, it is an interesting correlation that the police have taken a higher profile, providing a commentary not only on law and order but also on the broader moral economy. Senior officers contribute too—Manchester Chief Constable James Anderton constantly attacked homosexuals, once referring to AIDS as a 'cesspit of their own making', and Metropolitan Commissioner Kenneth Newman blamed the rise in crime on such diverse factors as television, left-wing politicians, and easy credit and claimed that the fragmentation of authority was encouraged by politicians who 'rather than appeal to the community as a whole, make a policy of appealing to the minorities in it. There have been recent examples of stances taken in order to appeal to sectarian, racial and sexual minorities.'[11]

Policing the Family

The 'private' lives that have so far been discussed have involved beliefs and actions that indirectly affect others: political opinion, moral and social beliefs, sexual orientation, drug-taking, being black, being a woman. They have also been private lives in public, not protected by private territory. The thesis has been that we fail to protect a realm of the 'private', immune from formal state regulation and intervention, despite the fact that it is a concept that permeates everyday thought.

Yet if we look closely, it appears that the police, while disregarding privacy in some instances, make it a useful argument for non-intervention in others. The definition of justifiable privacy in police terms reflects assumptions about structures of traditional control. The areas for non-intervention have traditionally been the workplace and the family. The organization of labour has resolved much of the exploitation of the former. Yet deaths through avoidable industrial accidents run into thousands and prosecutions for negligent manslaughter are unheard of.

The contradictions in police definitions of privacy are clearest of all in relation to the family. This is an area where the police are reluctant to intervene in one context yet very willing in another. For instance the family is where most of the physical and sexual abuse of women and children occurs. Although the wife is a regular murder victim, police still treat 'domestic disputes' as 'rubbish', unworthy of their time and attention. Many legal and occupational reasons can be advanced for this—until the Police and Criminal Evidence Act 1984 the wife was not even a compellable witness in court proceedings against her husband. Thus, if the police took action, there was a significant risk that their only witness would refuse to testify. Over-involvement might lead to complaints against the officer, and this, allied to the low status of such incidents, was a positive disincentive to becoming involved. The privacy of the home and of the marital relationship provided a good justification for non-intervention. The lack of protection afforded to the battered wife by the police was a direct cause of the growth of women's refuges in the 1970s.

The police still show little interest in elevating the problem of domestic violence to the front page, despite the obvious and immediate scale of the problem. In London in 1986 a report on police handling of the problem was left unpublished for nine months before being leaked to the press. For the police, the battered wife is an unimportant victim—further, within the machismo ethic of the police force, 'chastisement' is seen as normal. The battering husband presents no threat outside the home and is often a good neighbour and employee. To the public, the wife is often presented as 'deserving' her bruises.

Contradictorily, the police involvement with juveniles shows no such shyness at being involved in family relationships. The growth of juvenile bureaux within all forces in the 1970s has always been seen as a 'pro-active' (as opposed to a 'reactive') police measure. Direct involvement in the family, alongside other agencies, as a result of minor criminal offences or truancy is not precluded by some notion of the 'privacy' of the family home or of family relationships. Incidents are not left for the family to sort out themselves, although the police are sensitive to parental authority and seek to support it rather than undermine it. Juveniles, especially in urban settings, are seen as potential 'police problems' outside the home and the police have been successful in moulding opinion that this is a matter of 'law and order' and crime prevention. The disaffected working-class male presents a clear threat to established authority and no conceptions of privacy will prevent the police from making a detailed penetration of civil society to maintain a good flow of local intelligence and a level of control.

The concept of privacy is highly relativist, with the boundary between what is regulated and what is not, between intervention and immunity, moving back and forth across time. Nevertheless, the 'individual' remains the basic building block of the liberal state. The subject can make a claim to the right to personal privacy, and in everyday life people use 'privacy' as a concept that has meaning to them and through which they constitute their own identity and their relationships to others. Many states entrench such rights in their constitutions. Constitutional policing in this country must equally recognize them and give them due weight. The individual should be left unregulated except where there is some necessity for the State to intervene. The burden of justifying intervention has to be on the State. Such an abstract argument moves us no nearer the delimitation of what concretely constitutes necessity. Liberal theorists such as Hart,[12] arguing for the reform of the laws against homosexuality, have pointed to the need to establish identifiable harm to others as opposed to some collective moral interest. Such a formula would mean a narrower ambit for the criminal law and for the police, but a counter-argument might suggest that non-interventionist policies according high priority to private territory and relationships merely allow for greater exploitation and violence against the vulnerable and the powerless. This is a matter for discretion and flexibility of judgement: where actions directly affect others, the right to privacy can be forfeited. Obviously there can be a collective claim to privacy, by the family or an institution, but where the claim merely conceals the exploitation of one or more of the vulnerable members, for example the sexual assault of children, then it becomes unjustifiable. Collectively a liberal society must always intervene to prevent harm through exploitation, whether in the workplace, in the family, or in the market. The police role here, as everywhere, should be that of protectors of the community rather than attackers of individual rights and the embodiment of a traditional authority.

7

The Accountability of the Police

Recently the Police Complaints Authority have initiated investigations into incidents such as the shooting of Dennis Bergin at the Sir John Soane Museum in London in February 1987; the courts have dealt with prosecutions of police officers such as Inspector Lovelock, acquitted of wounding charges arising out of the shooting of Cherry Groce in Brixton in 1985; Manchester Local Police Authority (and the Home Office) have had heart-to-hearts with James Anderton over his public pronouncements; Metropolitan Commissioner Kenneth Newman announced an internal inquiry into the events on the picket lines at Wapping while MPs pressed for a parliamentary debate on the same topic.

This kaleidoscope prompts the questions, 'Who controls the police?' or 'To whom are they answerable?' Accountability implies some form of explanation and justification, usually a public one. It does not mean direction or control with operational policy being decided by some outside body. Control of day-to-day operations rests firmly with the Chief Constable, although he is subject to scrutiny and influence by the Home Office and the government. The examples above show an apparent breadth of police accountability, through formal and informal channels. They face a range of audiences—not merely the public and senior officers but local and national politicians, judges, the media, as well as a formal complaints procedure.

It is important that there are mechanisms through which people can obtain retrospective answers about the exercise of bureaucratic power—there is a sense of powerlessness and loss of self-determination in the face of institutions, whether educational, health, social services, or law and order. The development of overall policies for areas other than the police is often a political issue, but, unlike the police, their accountability is rarely seen as a major issue. But the effect on the individual can be as dramatic in, say, a hospital as in a police station. Deaths and serious injuries through medical malpractice will far outnumber deaths in police custody. The broad powers of the police and doctors pose similar problems of personal liberty, whether for the mentally handicapped or the suspect in the cells. Both occupations are jealous of their independence and professional autonomy. Both have internal complaints machineries which frequently give minimal satisfaction to complainants. Both are extremely powerful and effective lobby groups.

There is a distinction—we accept medical treatment voluntarily—but there is a significant parallel. Yet doctors are allowed considerably more self-policing, attract much less media attention, are generally seen as less politically sensitive, and are able to protect deviant members to a far greater extent. The police consider themselves more visible and more vulnerable to media scrutiny and appear more frequently on the political agenda. The inherent drama in crime and police work makes it much more attractive to newspapers than the work of, say, the social services. But media visibility is not the sole reason for debate over accountability, or football would undoubtedly possess independent tribunals and spectator-complaints machinery! Nor is it the functions carried out by the police: social workers and doctors probably affect individuals and the community as deeply. A partial explanation for recent concern is the growing alienation appearing between whole communities and the police. But, as has been stressed, the police do possess a symbolic importance, representing ideals of justice and the relationship between citizen and state that are of great significance. Failings of the police are highlighted which would go unremarked in other occupations.

As will appear, the techniques of accountability are frequently less effective than they seem. Nevertheless, the police establishment opposes reform, essentially on the ground that they are answerable to law. Senior policemen argue that democratic means of accountability lead to political control and that this would undermine police neutrality in social conflict. Political interference can only subvert the objective of maintaining balance and the common good. There is a parallel claim for independence by doctors, whose defence of their 'clinical judgement' enables them to retain an autonomy of decision-making, even in those areas, such as abortions or neo-natal deaths of handicapped children, where the basis of judgement is not wholly scientific but incorporates personal and moral values. Operational decisions by the police can be similar, but even those chief officers, such as John Alderson in Devon and Cornwall who promoted 'community policing' were wholly against democratic control. Communities might be consulted and liaised with but the benevolent social policing was to be by an undemocratic, non-accountable police force.

I will return to the 'legal or democratic' debate but will first examine the different types of accountability.

Accountability by Newspaper

Twenty-five per cent of all copy in newspapers comprises law-and-order news—the figure is higher in the tabloids, although the *Daily Telegraph* devotes more column inches to this issue than any other paper. The police organize their relationships to the media in a highly professional manner and journalists rely on their police contacts to provide interviews, information, and interpretations. To present alternative versions is to risk such sources drying up. In Northern Ireland, interviewing the IRA or pursuing independent lines of investigation can lead to non-co-operation from the police or the withdrawal of press cards. While he was Commissioner of the Metropolitan Police, Robert Mark introduced identification cards for press access to the Old Bailey—withdrawal was an obvious sanction against recalcitrant journalists. Television documentaries or programmes such as ITV's *Police 5* or the BBC's *Crimewatch* also depend on police co-operation. The BBC, after a series of plays called *Law and Order* which presented a jaundiced view of the entire criminal justice system but especially of the violence and corruption endemic in the Metropolitan force, now permit Scotland Yard to comment on (and by implication edit) news items, documentaries, and plays that concern them.

The police believe that the media are over-critical. Robert Mark complained in 1974 that the police were 'the most abused, the most unfairly criticised and the most silent minority in this country'. But most of the time the press are willing allies in the law-and-order discourse—that is, the assumptions about the 'problems' of crime, about who represents the 'dangerous classes' about 'proper' sanctions. Stuart Hall's[1] analysis of the press coverage of the 'mugging' panic of 1973–4 is a compelling illustration of co-operation between police, press, and judges in the manufacture of a crime wave (despite the flimsy statistical basis), of the image of the unsafe streets, of the stereotype of the young black mugger (ignoring the preceding disastrous breakdown of police relationships with black communities), and of the call for stiff, deterrent sentences.

But from time to time investigative journalism and news photography present telling evidence or dramatic images of malpractice. The level of corruption in the Metropolitan force was revealed in a front-page story in *The Times* in 1969,[2] using the transcript of a tape-recording of a police sergeant asking a suspect for money. Revelations in the *People* followed in 1972 about the dubious practices of the Drugs Squad and the rake-offs from Soho pornographers enjoyed by the Obscene Publications Squad. These stories led to the installation of Robert Mark as Metropolitan Police Commissioner. Coming from Leicester, he was appointed as a man untainted by the Met's history. It was Mark who developed an internal investigation unit with substantial muscle, A10 (now CIB2), especially to bring CID under control. But although the campaign to clean up the Metropolitan force has continued, it has had little success. The difficulties were exemplified by Frank Williamson, an HMI brought in to investigate the original allegations in *The Times*. Leading the inquiry for the Yard was the Head of the Obscene Publications Squad, Bill Moody, to be convicted of corruption himself in 1977. Williamson abandoned not only the inquiry but also the police service as he believed that neither Scotland Yard nor the Home Office were willing to instigate the necessary reform of the Metropolitan force. The story was to be repeated with 'Operation Countryman' in the early 1980s.

Sometimes newspaper campaigns meet with more success—in August 1983 a police Transit van drew up by a bus-stop in the Holloway Road and five youths were beaten up by police officers. At first no policeman would identify the culprits, but the persistence of press coverage of the story led to the prosecution and dismissal of the officers involved. Conversely, despite continuing newspaper coverage, no SPG officer has ever been prosecuted or disciplined for Blair Peach's death in 1979, although Commander Cass's internal report clearly identified the officers involved and apparently recommended prosecution, not only for homicide but for riot, affray, and conspiracy to pervert the course of justice.

This instance illustrates the limits of newspaper coverage: the media have no formal status, their methods of acquiring evidence and their type of approach can be easily attacked, and the police are under no obligation to answer press questions. Usually the news value of any story is of short duration and will last a few issues at most. Television reporting is even shorter and news programmes rarely follow up particular items on successive days. Documentary series such as *Panorama*, *World in Action*, or *Diverse Reports* might devote a single programme to an investigation in depth—racialist arson attacks in Walthamstow, the police tactics employed during the Home Secretary's visit to Manchester University or on the Orgreave picket line during the miners' strike. It is ephemeral, valued or despised by those with an interest, but for the majority insignificant when contrasted with the favourable and glamorous coverage of the 'war against crime' in daily newspapers.

Accountability at Law

The police consistently argue that the limits of their powers and their procedures are defined by legal rules. They see themselves first and foremost as accountable to the courts for their actions. But their decisions and policies are characterized as much by discretion as by rules. Good policing is a matter not of going by the book but of principles of fairness which cannot be effectively adjudicated in a court of law.

Naturally individuals can seek redress through the courts—with criminal prosecutions for assault; with civil suits against officers or the Local Police Authority for compensation for wrongful detention or under the Fatal Accident Acts.[3] Solicitors often advise their clients to bypass the formal complaints machinery which is rarely satisfactory, and to sue immediately. These sorts of case are normally the result of excesses by individual officers and are not considered further. In 1986 the mother of a victim of the Yorkshire Ripper sought to establish a broader ground of police liability, suing for damages and alleging that her daughter would not have died but for the negligent performance of the police in investigating these killings. It was

accepted that there were major errors of judgement and ineffi-
ciencies, but the Court of Appeal held that although the police had a
general duty to suppress crime, there was no liability to individuals
for negligent failure to carry out that duty.[4]

It is the need to expose and analyse the general policies followed by
any force that is at the heart of accountability. They can often be
examined and influenced through court actions such as those men-
tioned above, but there are also other methods—first, indirectly
through the operation of the exclusionary rule of evidence, and second, by a direct challenge to a particular policy by judicial review. A
third and new form of accountability through the legal process has
recently arisen with the creation in 1986 of the Crown Prosecution
Service.

The Exclusionary Rule

One technique for influencing police behaviour is the court's power
to exclude evidence improperly or illegally obtained.[5] The Cali-
fornian police provided a dramatic illustration of this in the 1930s
when they pumped out the contents of a suspect's stomach in the
belief that he had swallowed drugs. They sought, but were not permitted, to introduce the stomach contents as evidence. In England
the examples are usually less dramatic: the seizure of incriminating
material from a suspect's house when no magistrate's warrant has
been obtained, excessive periods of interrogation, or perhaps the
planting of a police informer in a suspect's cell. Excluding evidence
gained by such means increases the possibility of an acquittal, which
in turn would lead to internal review and the possibility of proper
procedures being observed in the future. The American Supreme
Court actively polices the police through these methods, especially
through the interpretation of the Fourth Amendment to the Constitution, which prohibits unlawful search and seizure of evidence, and
through seminal decisions, such as that in *Miranda* v. *Arizona*[6] in
1966 which treated as inadmissible evidence a confession obtained
in the absence of a caution. The central question is whether such
decisions in fact affect police behaviour. It remains debatable.
But excluding evidence signals the critical importance of procedural
justice in maintaining civil rights.

The exclusionary rule is much narrower in the United Kingdom
than it is in the US. Judges have been cautious in expanding the rule,

although with confessions there is a long tradition that incriminating statements made by the accused are not admissible evidence if they have been obtained by some hope of advantage or duress, and this has now been put in statutory form through s. 74 of the Police and Criminal Evidence Act 1984. In 1987, in the trial arising out of the killing of PC Blakelock at Broadwater Farm in 1985, a juvenile was acquitted when it emerged that he had been interviewed for three days, clad in his underpants and a blanket: the judge refused to accept that the confession that emerged was reliable evidence. Despite this apparent protection, the judicial record in safeguarding the rights of defendants is patchy, even when confessions have been obtained by oppressive interrogation and violence—in 1975 six men were convicted of the Birmingham pub bombings, partly on the evidence of confessions beaten out of them by the West Midlands police, despite the fact that the beatings were readily apparent at their preliminary appearances in the magistrates' court.[7]

But apart from confessions there is no automatic exclusion of the evidence obtained by improper police practices. It was generally believed that the judges had discretion to exclude evidence obtained by improper means. In *Allen* (1977)[8] the judge refused to accept statements made after the defendant had been refused access to a solicitor. Such cases are notable for their rarity. More common is the type of decision by Widgery LCJ in *Jeffery* v. *Black*:[9] the suspect was arrested in a pub, accused of having stolen and half-eaten a sandwich. The police insisted on his accompanying them to his flat which, without a warrant and without his consent, they proceeded to search. The small amount of cannabis that was found was admitted in evidence and the defendant was convicted of possession of drugs.

Judges have always adhered to the basic rule that if evidence is relevant and reliable, then it should be admitted in evidence and it is not the court's job to maintain proper standards of police behaviour. The major exception to such a position was under the drink/driving laws in the 1960s and 1970s where a procedural failure by a constable would lead to evidence of intoxication being rejected and convictions quashed. But in the arena of the 'true' criminal law, this has never happened—in *Sang*,[10] a decision in the House of Lords in 1980, the defendant argued that he had been inveigled into the offence by an *agent provocateur* working on behalf of the police. The court first laid down that there was no defence of entrapment known to English law—that is, if the police secretly encourage you to commit an offence, this is not a ground for acquittal. But further the Lords ruled that the trial judge does not have a general discretion (apart from the area of confessions) to refuse evidence that has been obtained by improper or unfair means.

The Police and Criminal Evidence Act 1984 has reintroduced this discretion in s. 78. Judges may reject improperly obtained evidence but only if it will have an adverse effect on the fairness of the proceedings—that is, the judge must ask not whether the police action was justified, but whether the fairness of the trial will be affected. It is possible that future courts will interpret this provision broadly, but it is unlikely. Another consequence of the 1984 Act was the promulgation of four Codes of Conduct for the police, detailing matters such as the conditions of detention and interrogation and exact procedures for identification parades. Trial courts are now hearing arguments from the defence that evidence obtained in breach of the codes should be rejected.

Controlling Operational Policy

People who disagree with or are adversely affected by a decision of a tribunal or government agency can apply to the High Court for a review of that decision. The Divisional Court of Queen's Bench has the power to order a public body to act where it has failed to take action or to cease from activity where it is acting beyond its powers, or to quash decisions. It is a process not of appeal on the facts or the law but of review; that is, it decides whether the body has acted outside its powers or in an improper fashion. This has obvious applications for anyone concerned with general policing policy and not solely with a specific abuse.

But this judicial power is rarely exercised—in 1973 in *Blackburn (No. 3)*[11] the applicant sought an order of *mandamus* against the Metropolitan Police to compel them to enforce the provisions of the Obscene Publications Act against certain Soho sex shops. Lord Denning held that the chief officer had broad discretion as to the deployment of his constables and that this was not a situation where the court would interfere with the exercise of that discretion.

The same approach was used in *ex parte Central Electricity Generating Board* (1981)[12] where the CEGB were being prevented from carrying out a survey on the site of a projected nuclear power station in Cornwall by the owners of the land and a crowd of demonstrators. The Chief Constable, John Alderson, refused to disperse the crowd, feeling that he lacked the necessary powers and that such an action would harm police–public relations. The Court of Appeal held that the police did have powers of dispersal in such a situation and obviously felt that John Alderson should exercise them. But it still refused to grant the order requested by the CEGB. Lord Denning said, 'It was of first importance that the police should decide on their own responsibility what action should be taken in any particular situation.'

The judges have reserved a residual power of intervention. They have never said that the police are not subject to the authority of the court. *Ex parte Levy* (1985)[13] arose when the Chief Constable of Liverpool, Kenneth Oxford, instructed his officers not to enter the Toxteth area of Liverpool in police vehicles. The applicant had had property stolen and the thieves were being pursued by a police car which stopped the chase when it approached Toxteth. Although the case was resolved on different issues, Watkins LJ looked at the policy and concluded that it was in line with the Scarman recommendations and that the Chief Constable was justified in adopting such measures. The court in this instance was much more concerned with the substance of the policy than with the formal principle of not interfering with the exercise of discretion.

The Discretion to Prosecute

A further method of using the legal process to check on police behaviour can be the decision whether to prosecute. Until 1986 this decision was in the hands of the police themselves. Almost all forces had a prosecuting solicitors department, often at headquarters. Under the new arrangements there now exists an independent Crown Prosecution Service under the Director of Public Prosecutions and the Attorney-General.

The decision to prosecute is central, since an individual case may exemplify a general policy by the police to lay charges resulting from, say, all incidents of soliciting in public lavatories or disturbances on a picket line. Alternatively, the police themselves may have breached the codes of conduct in the course of an investigation. As we have seen, the courts will not concern themselves with such issues. However, the creation of the independent prosecution service adds another layer of accountability since the prosecutor must be satisfied that there is evidence on which a court might properly convict. But it is difficult to see that the prosecutors' discretion will not stretch somewhat further—since the CPS has to accept the criticism for unjustified prosecution, it will inevitably seek closer control as to which prosecutions proceed.

Local Police Authorities

The development of the small local force in the nineteenth century meant substantial control by local landed and business élites who, from the Municipal Corporations Act 1835, composed the Watch Committees in the boroughs and, after the Local Government Act 1888, composed the Standing Joint Committees in the counties (prior to this, the shire forces had been directly under magisterial control). Interference with the policies pursued by the force was common—Brogden[14] gives the example of the Liverpool Watch Committee in 1890 compelling its chief officer, Nott-Bower, into action against the brothels. Local control in the nineteenth century was very strong and provides no support for current arguments which would treat police independence as existing since 1829.[15]

The twentieth century has seen a significant decline in local control with a corresponding increase in the independence, power, and prestige of the Chief Constable. Bunyan[16] has argued that this decline can be correlated with the increasing enfranchisement of the working class which culminated in the vote being given to women in 1928. The decades after the First World War saw a build-up in the position of the Chief Constable in order to counter 'meddlesome Socialist local bodies'. Treating the police as independent avoided the inevitable local opposition that would arise from creating a 'national' force, yet ensured that Home Office influence would be a central factor, given the background of the senior police officers.

This reconstruction of the constitutional position of the police was given an additional boost by the decision in *Fisher* v. *Oldham Corporation*,[17] where the plaintiff, wrongfully arrested and detained by police officers, sought damages from the town as the constables' employer. It was decided by McCardie J that the constable exercised independent powers arising from his office and conferred upon him by common law or statute. The local authority could not interfere with the exercise of such a public power—there was no master–servant relationship between the officer and the town. This was not an appellate decision but it has been used to justify the decrease in local-authority control. Lustgarten argues that this extrapolation from the constable's exercise of the power of arrest to a chief officer's decision about the operational policies of the force as a whole is wholly unjustified. The modern police force's independence of local authorities has no historical or legal basis.

The relationship between the local authority and its police was established by the powers conferred on the Local Police Authorities created by the Police Act 1964. But the Act and the Royal Commission preceding it were the result of confrontations between Watch Committees and their Chief Constables, with corruption scandals in Worcester and Brighton and incompetence alleged against the senior Cardigan officers. But the most notorious concerned the Chief Constable of Nottingham, Captain Popkess, whose enquiries into local-authority corruption led to the Watch Committee demanding reports on his investigation. Insisting that law enforcement was the province of the chief officer and not of the Watch Committee, he refused, was dismissed and reinstated, but soon retired.

His view of the relationship between the local authority and the Chief Constable was endorsed by the Police Act. S. 5 of the Act put the responsibility for 'direction and control' of the force into the hands of the Chief Constable but left (s. 4) the maintenance of an 'adequate and efficient' force as the job of the police authorities which took over from the Watch Committees and the Standing Joint Committees.

There are differing types of local police authority. In London there is no LPA at all and the authority for the metropolitan forces is still the Home Secretary—the Metropolitan force was castigated by the chairman of the GLC's Police Committee (an unofficial body) as being the most expensive and least efficient in the country, with the lowest level of public confidence.[18] London ratepayers contribute £400 million to the Metropolitan Police budget, with no control on how it is spent.

In the provinces the standard model is the force based upon county boundaries, either shire or metropolitan, with the police authority consisting of magistrates and councillors. The LPA is a sub-committee of the full council but is differentiated from other local-authority services in that the full council does not have the power to overturn decisions except on matters of finance.

However, there are also ten forces which are an amalgamation of counties, such as Devon and Cornwall or Thames Valley. The police authority members are drawn from the relevant local authorities. Here the LPA is wholly independent and does not have to weigh police demands against competing claims for resources. They present the constituent local authorities with a rate demand which those authorities have no power to refuse.

There are now also combined local police authorities for conurbations such as Merseyside and Greater Manchester. Since the abolition of the metropolitan county councils in 1985 the police authority has been a joint board comprised of nominees of the district councils, but the budget and establishment have to be approved by the Secretary of State. After a period of three years the individual councils can, again with the approval of the Home Secretary, leave the combined force and set up independently. This has led to the reformation of Merseyside and Greater Manchester LPAs, both of which had engaged in a bitter struggle with their Chief Constables.

The powers of the LPAs are quite limited. For ten years after the 1964 legislation they were content to leave the precise demarcation boundaries obscure. Operational issues were the responsibility of the Chief Constable and the authorities were essentially the quartermasters. The LPA is responsible for the appointment of the Chief Constable but this has to be approved by the Home Secretary and the LPA makes its choice from a short-list drawn up by the Home Office. Its powers to dismiss the Chief Constable are equally circumscribed. The LPA is able to decide the overall establishment of the force, to provide vehicles and other equipment, as well as to determine the overall budget. The Chief Constable has a statutory duty to present an annual report to the LPA, and it is also able to request (but not require) a report on any matter concerning policing in the area. The Chief Constable can refuse to produce such a report if he feels that it is not in the public interest or within the LPA's proper province. This province is frequently defined by Chief Constables as excluding matters of operational policing. In the event of a refusal to furnish a report the LPA can appeal to the Home Secretary, but if he upholds the Chief Constable there is nothing further that it can do.

LPAs have attempted to play a more positive role in recent years:

on Merseyside Kenneth Oxford was cross-examined on the death of Jimmy Kelly in police custody and was later censured for unauthorized expenditure on riot-control equipment; James Anderton in Greater Manchester was prevented from reading a report on the 1981 riots as well as taken to task for purchasing CS gas and sub-machineguns; in Leicester concern was expressed about racialism within the force, while in London local councils have sought to influence policing policy: after certain National Front rallies in South London Lewisham threatened not to pay the policing precept without some commitment to a form of ratepayer scrutiny. The lack of consultation has led many London boroughs (as well as other metropolitan areas) to organize permanent independent police committees.

The miners' strike in 1984–5 highlighted several problems with regard to the relationship between local police authorities, Chief Constables, and the Home Office.[19] The manpower for the operations was provided under the 'mutual aid' provisions of the Police Act 1964. S. 14 empowers Chief Constables to provide assistance to other forces when requested. If they refuse, the Home Secretary has the power to order that such assistance be given. The original legislation in 1890 made this a matter for the police authority, but nowadays, in Lustgarten's terms, 'it merely picks up the tab'. LPAs, even those unwilling to be involved in operational matters, had seen themselves as the financial watchdogs of policing, responsible to the ratepayers for the 50 per cent of the police budget that comes directly from local rates. Of course, the divide between operational and financial issues is far from exact. A budget can merely be a financial ceiling within which the Chief Constable operates. But the police authority should be aware of the categories of expenditure to ensure that its duties under s. 4 (providing an adequate and efficient force) are being carried out—the type of equipment which is being purchased[20] (helicopters or CS gas) or the amount of the contribution to the costs of the regional crime squad. The need for approval obfuscates the boundary between the financial and the operational.

At the time of the miners' strike, the Home Secretary had an early meeting with Chief Constables and told them not to allow financial constraints to interfere with the 'operational discharge of your duties'. This action was taken without the knowledge of LPAs, who found in many instances that their own forces had been decimated in order to provide assistance in other parts of the country. Other authorities discovered that they had spent millions of pounds in obtaining that assistance. Initially this bill was to be paid by the local ratepayers. For many councils, the extra expenditure created worse problems in that it took them over the rate-capping limits imposed by central government, with the consequent financial penalties.

The LPAs engaged in a range of tactics to force the Home Office into treating the issue as a national one and thus providing a higher proportion of the costs out of central funds. Derbyshire wrote to the LPAs of aiding forces (providing assistance at a cost of £120,000 a day) explaining that it had no intention of paying. Yet those LPAs could not prevent those officers from being sent. When South Yorkshire refused to pay for billetting the constables required for policing the Orgreave coking plant, the Attorney-General immediately initiated a court action to quash their decision and to get the authority to comply with its 'obligations' under the Police Act. However, the action never came to court as the Home Secretary provided further financial assistance to the South Yorkshire authority.

A different tactic was to cut police budgets in other, often sensitive, areas. South Yorkshire attracted Home Office criticism and threatened legal action when it maintained its school-crossing patrol but cut its police horses and dogs. James Anderton of Greater Manchester protested loudly when the LPA cut the police band (which included several full-time officers), but this time the Home Office proffered no support. Nor did it carry out another threat to take legal action when Nottinghamshire withdrew from the regional crime squad.

It was a period which showed the limits of LPA powers, even over finance. The so-called tripartite system of police government looked fragile. The Home Secretary and the Association of Chief Police Officers had a clear policy towards the policing of the strike. But the local authorities were excluded from the formulation of the policy and found themselves in debt for bills over which they had no control. The tripartite system had given way to control shared between the Home Office and the Chief Constables.

The Home Office and Central Direction

The decline in local influence has been accompanied by a corresponding increase in the power of senior police officers and of the Home Office. Facilities are increasingly provided on a national basis, whether the forensic science laboratories, the National Police Computer at Hendon, or national and regional training centres.

The Home Secretary also has certain statutory powers—for example, s. 32 of the Police Act 1964 gives him the power to institute an inquiry into policing matters. The Scarman Report on the Brixton riots was an inquiry of this kind, as was the investigation into the interrogation techniques of Detective Sergeant Challenor in Sheffield in the 1960s. But this and other powers exercised by the Home Secretary are specific ones granted to him by the various Police Acts. There is no residual power to take over the management of a particular force if it is being run in a manner that the Home Secretary finds unreasonable. This is almost certainly unnecessary since existing powers and less direct influences allow the Home Office to intervene in policy and management issues in an immediate and effective way.

But the growth in Home Office influence has not been matched by any increase in parliamentary scrutiny. Ministers answer to Parliament for those matters for which they have responsibility but as the Home Secretary has no direct constitutional link to the provincial forces, MPs' questions relating to such forces will go unanswered. Although he is the police authority for London, questions here will prove equally fruitless: being usually defined as 'operational policy', they are a matter for the Commissioner. Lustgarten[21] argues that while operational decisions rest on the experience and competence of police officers, they inevitably have a substantial political content since they represent particular choices for the community—the 'hard' or 'soft' style of policing, involvement in industrial disputes, specific emphasis on areas of concern, or the acquisition of new arsenals or computers. In such decisions the local community has virtually no say through its councillors. Nor does the MP have any impact.

The influence of the Home Office and its refusal to accept responsibility were shown in 1972, when the Illegal Immigration Unit was set up as a result of a Home Office initiative. At the time the Minister concerned, Mark Carlisle, refused to answer parliamentary questions, alleging that it was an operational decision for the chief officers concerned and not subject to parliamentary control. In 1973 the Immigration Unit mounted a raid in Camden, designed to examine passports and catch aliens without proper documentation. A Home Office circular a few months before had stressed that the Draconian powers of the 1971 Immigration Act would not be used for fishing expeditions of this nature, yet the Home Secretary still declined to answer questions in Parliament.

As was described in Chapter 2, a separate police department was set up in the Home Office following the passage of the Police Act in 1919. This Act also gave the Home Secretary the power to promulgate disciplinary and other regulations regarding conditions of service for police officers and thus promote a certain uniformity among forces. For county forces, such control had existed since the 1856 County and Borough Police Act which also established Her Majesty's Inspectorate of Constabulary. The Inspectorate remains a critical conduit between the local force and the Home Office, although it has little contact with local police authorities. Each of the five inspectors with an administrative staff is attached to a region and carries out periodic inspections within it, as well as receiving regular reports from the forces. He also acts as convener and chairman of the regional conferences of Chief Constables and promotes inter-force collaboration, particularly through the regional crime squads. He reports directly to the Home Office and his findings are not made available to LPAs.

The threat to withhold the central grant is another potential lever over policing policy. LPAs and Chief Constables are ill-placed to resist the Home Secretary's wishes since the block grant amounts to some millions of pounds: under recent rate-capping schemes it would be prohibitively expensive to fund policing solely from local rates. The threat may have been used quite frequently—although Brogden[22] gives York and Stockport in 1965 as the most recent examples, Critchley[23] suggests that on average the threat is made every two years. But how real are these threats? Home Secretary Leon Brittan threatened legal action against LPAs which proposed cuts in police budgets as a result of the costs of the miners' strike, but such action was in fact never taken. Would it be politically feasible to impose withholding of the block grant over South Yorkshire police horses or the Manchester Police band?

New ideas emerge from the centre: in 1984 the chief HMI suggested that greater emphasis should be given to the work of the drugs squads; in 1987 a Home Office working party recommended the development of specialist firearms units for all forces. A determined Chief Constable backed by his LPA might well resist such pressure if there were different operational priorities for that particular force.

John Alderson showed such determination in introducing community policing schemes in Devon and Cornwall.

But divergences of opinion over central issues are unlikely; not only does the Home Office provide the short-list of applicants for posts of Chief Constable, but all such applicants will have been through the senior command courses at the National Police College at Bramshill. The commandant at Bramshill is himself one of the most senior officers in the country, alongside the Metropolitan Police Commissioner and the head of the Inspectorate of Constabulary. Regular regional and national conferences of Chief Constables as well as the operation of the Association of Chief Police Officers mean that at senior management level there is a broad consensus on major policy.

The Home Office informs local forces of its views by advisory circulars of which there are about 100 a year. These circulars, though advisory in name, are essentially mandatory. They are frequently the result of liaison between the Home Office and ACPO. Although Chief Constables cavil occasionally they treat circulars as commands. But they are not the result of any form of democratic consultation and LPAs are given no right to see them, even though the policy advanced might directly impinge on their financial responsibilities. Nor is there any means for Parliament to discuss these circulars.

The image of local independence and diversity suggested by the formal organization of the police is dispelled by an examination of the working practices. The move towards centralism was taken further, as we have seen, by the establishment of the National Reporting Centre in 1972. During the miners' strike LPAs saw executive control vested in the NRC—the chairman of the South Yorkshire LPA, George Moores, is quoted as saying: 'You see, the National Reporting Centre is *the authority that has directed the number of policemen we need* and as a consequence we have no control over the budget.' Lustgarten has suggested that the NRC lets the Home Office off the ideological and political hook, retaining the myth of the apolitical nature of policing while achieving the precise political objectives desired.

Most European countries have national policing with political control vested in a ministry, answerable to some democratic process. In the United Kingdom we have moved towards a system which is amenable to a high degree of central influence and control but lacks genuine democratic accountability. The 'tripartite' system has only two full partners, with occasional genuflections towards the local authority. There is a conflict between police independence, democratic accountability, and local character. The conflict might be solved were LPAs elected and given enhanced powers of appointment and dismissal of senior ranks, subject to a Home Office veto for which the Home Secretary would be answerable in Parliament. To ensure real local involvement, police authorities should have more power to discuss and decide operational priorities, to exercise proper financial controls, to supervise a local complaints machinery, and to establish closer liaison with the inspectorate. All of this could quite easily be subject to direction by the Home Office if the powers were used unreasonably.

Monitoring and Liaison Groups

Attempts by local people to be involved in policing issues are a phenomenon of the last ten years. This development is relatively late in an era which has seen the rise of activist pressure groups on a range of issues. Policing, unlike issues such as disarmament, poverty, racialism, or even prisons, remained uncontroversial for a long period after World War II. But since the late 1970s two types of organization have emerged. First are groups with a critical and reformist approach, which have sought to monitor police actions and produce alternative information for the media. Several sprang up during the miners' strike, others have looked at deaths in police custody or the operation of the identification laws. Most common are bodies based on a neighbourhood, often funded by the local authority, of which some have developed into fully fledged pressure groups, such as the GLC Police Committee which campaigned vigorously against the Police and Criminal Evidence Act. With the abolition of the GLC, many London boroughs have created their own committees.

The second form of organization has developed from police initiatives—'community liaison' has had a higher priority for them in the 1980s. Local officers may hold informal meetings with local residents to identify anxieties about crime and explain the actions that the police can or cannot take. My local paper reported such a meeting in a small Kent village where the audience were told that they could no longer expect instant response to calls about burglaries: if the burglar was not on the premises, then it mattered little whether the police arrived within twenty minutes or twenty hours. Demands on police time inevitably meant that they had to give different priorities to calls for assistance. Such meetings have often been convened to expand the Neighbourhood Watch scheme.

In response to the Scarman recommendations, more formal liaison committees have been set up with representatives from a range of local groups and associations. Under the Police and Criminal Evidence Act 1984, s. 106, liaison committees were made compulsory for all forces and the police authorities were obliged to organize them (except in London where that duty fell to the Metropolitan Police Commissioner). A Home Office circular in 1982 said that such groups were to identify local concerns about crime, to educate the public about the limits of policing, to stress the community's part in preventing crime, and to increase the consensual quality of policing. Unlike the monitoring bodies, these objectives take for granted the underlying aims and functions of policing and see liaison committees as assisting at the interface between the police and the public, making the police more acceptable but not seeking to discuss or influence policing policy. During the miners' strike, when the Canterbury area liaison committee sought to discuss the policing of the Kent mines, this was ruled to be outside the committee's terms of reference. Monitoring groups take the opposite view that policing itself is part of the problem of law and order.

The Individual Complaint

For the police officer and the citizen, the issue is often not general policy but is more akin to a private dispute where the plaintiff/citizen complains of the defendant/officer's behaviour. Over the past twenty years the chief objection to the existing complaints machinery has been that it leaves the investigation and adjudication of the complaint to officers from the same force—it is the guards who guard the guards. This was laid down by s. 49 of the Police Act 1964: the only independent element was the role of the Director of Public Prosecutions (DPP), who had to decide whether or not an allegation of crime against an officer should be prosecuted.

In the 1960s American forces experimented with independent civilian review boards, but these boards have now largely disappeared owing to the opposition of rank and file officers.[24] In Britain, some reform came through the Police Act 1976, though not without the resentment of the Police Federation and the retirement of Sir Robert Mark from his post of Metropolitan Commissioner. Its major innovation was the Police Complaints Board, an independent body which looked at all reports of investigations into complaints except those involving possible criminal charges, which still went to the DPP. The Board had no power or staff to carry out its own investigations and so the system still rested on the police's enquiries. However, the Board could request further information and advise that disciplinary action be taken.

The system did not inspire great public confidence—a 1981 survey[25] revealed that as many as 2 to 3 per cent of respondents believed that they had been the victims of illegal police behaviour and yet none had made a complaint, believing that 'nothing would be done' and that 'it was a waste of time'. Many solicitors shared this view. The widespread demand for an increased independent element continued, although the police themselves consistently argued that the internal approach was much more efficient, as junior officers were more likely to respond to their seniors than they were to an outsider. Certainly Mark's thoroughgoing anti-corruption purge by A10 led to massive resignations and early retirements. Active management can ensure an adequate system, although in recent years corruption scandals and allegations of freemasonry influence still dog the London force—in October 1986 the Chief Constable of South Yorkshire was named to head yet another inquiry.

If lack of independent investigation was seen as one defect of the 1976 system, so was the requirement that under the Act Chief Constables should record and appoint an investigating officer for all complaints. This led to a host of trivial matters being dealt with formally. Statistically there was a high increase in the number of complaints withdrawn, partly for this reason. A further factor may have been that under s. 44 (1) of the Police Act 1964 it had always been understood that the Police Federation could not use their funds to support officers in bringing legal action against complainants. Merlyn Rees, Home Secretary in 1976, in a palliative for the Police Federation, announced that his interpretation of s. 44 was different and that Federation funds might be used for this purpose. In addition, constables were given the right to see copies of the complaints made against them. As a result complainants are handed a leaflet warning that action may be taken against malicious or defamatory complaints. A final weakness was the lack of fair procedures for officers who were the subjects of complaints, whether these came from the public or were generated internally.

The police's own resentment died away as it became apparent that the Police Complaints Board were not rocking the boat and almost invariably supported police action. The DPP's office also gave the police little cause for concern, recommending prosecutions of officers in only 2 per cent of the cases referred to them. The weakness of the system was brought out by the Home Office Research Unit whose report (never published but leaked to *The Times* in 1981) severely criticized the Metropolitan force's manner of dealing with complaints of assault, suggesting that the inquiry was too often concerned with the criminal guilt or untrustworthiness of the complainant, too little with determining the facts. Overall investigations were inadequate and superficial. The 1981 inner-city disorders and the disquiet of many local police authorities also led to the mooting of new approaches—Merseyside LPA and Paul Boateng of the GLC Police Committee argued for greater democratic control of the police, elsewhere Alf Dubs, the MP, was putting forward a scheme for a full-scale police ombudsman with an investigative team independent of the police. The attractions of reform which would stave off more radical proposals became apparent to senior officers.

In 1984 the Police and Criminal Evidence Act produced a detailed scheme whereby, although complaints are all recorded, there is no need to appoint an investigating officer if the matter can be resolved informally by an explanation or an apology. If the matter is pursued formally, then an officer is appointed to investigate—normally from the same force, but if the complaint is serious, is an issue of public concern, or is against an officer of the rank of superintendent or higher, then from another force. The investigation is supervised by the Police Complaints Authority which has superseded the Police Complaints Board. The initial chairman of the PCA was a former Ombudsman, Sir Cecil Clothier. The Authority has the power to approve the choice of investigating officer and can insist on an officer of its own choosing. Furthermore, there is a supervisor from within the ranks of the PCA: in October 1986 Peter Wright, Chief Constable of South Yorkshire, was named to head the investigation of allegations of corruption within the Metropolitan force and

Roland Moyle, deputy chairman of the PCA, was appointed to supervise it.

All complaints within certain categories (including death and assault) will be referred to the Authority, but it also has the power to deal with other categories of complaint and with matters that are not the subject of a complaint at all—the mistaken shooting of Stephen Waldorf in 1983 by London officers hunting for David Martin, believed to have shot at the police, was treated by the Police Complaints Board as a complaint although they only had a single witness statement. However, the ambit of the Authority still excludes (by s. 84 (5) of the 1984 Act) issues of operational policy, although these may be of more significance than the excesses of individual officers.

The impact of this new system is uncertain—certainly the protection it gives the police in terms of rights to representation and appeal is long overdue. But there is more doubt about its effect on the low level of substantiated complaints—nineteen complaints out of twenty are regarded as unsubstantiated. One problem is always that of evidence, and as in all professions the police ranks close when a member is threatened. It is hard to find officers to testify against their colleagues.

Although the PCA publicly announce inquiries, for example into the Peace Convoy affair in 1985 or the shooting of Dennis Bergin in London in 1987, their effectiveness is minimal. Their investigations can take up to two years and then they only publish an annual report, not detailed individual reports. An exception to this was the inquiry into the Manchester Tactical Aid Group's operation at the University Students' Union in 1985. There was a fifteen-month investigation into 33 individual complaints and 71 general complaints about police conduct. Fifty-six police officers were interviewed under caution and 700 statements were taken. An eight-page summary was published in 1987. Only 3 officers were to be prosecuted, 2 for perjury and one for assault, despite videotapes of officers throwing students down stone steps. The PCA's main finding was that of serious mismanagement of the affair but the DPP prevented publication of any criticism of police tactics, claiming that it would prejudice the prosecution of the officers. The outcome was that the 'critical views of the authority' would be discussed with the two senior officers responsible for the operation. It begins to look as if the PCA will have a low public profile like its predecessor and have as little effect on police misconduct.

There is a wide spectrum of influences and pressures upon the police. But with the exception of the Home Office, from the viewpoint of the consumer of police services they all lack the power to change police practices or even to influence them significantly. The autonomy of the police is strengthened by the very multiplicity of possible approaches as well as by the limited scope, lack of access to information, and restricted powers of agencies such as the LPAs. Any review is bound to conclude that the 'governance' of the police is firmly vested in the hands of the Chief Constables and the Home Secretary and that the democratic and legal mechanisms which should exist in a liberal democracy to make them account for their decisions and the exercise of their power, are woefully absent. There is little justification for treating police services as different from health or education services, which are subject to constitutional safeguards. Indeed, there is every reason why the safeguards should be even stronger.

8

Conclusion—
a Constitutional Police?

The Control of Power

What are the elements of 'constitutionalism'? For liberal theory, control of power is a central theme. Within authoritarian regimes, economic and political power is wielded for the benefit of, say, a feudal élite, a racial grouping, or a military dictatorship, without regard to minority interests. The liberal state avoids this, first by formally separating the political from the economic by democratic mechanisms, but also by imposing checks on that political power—classically by distinguishing and separating the legislative, judicial, and executive functions. Unlike the US, Britain blurs these 'checks and balances'—through the doctrine of parliamentary supremacy, cabinet government has considerable potential for imposing a political programme, albeit constitutionally.

Whatever its precise form, Marxist theory sees liberal ideology and systems of government as a smokescreen. The rhetoric of individual rights and the limits of the state is perceived as a political scaffolding which conceals and reinforces the essential economic structures and dominant mode of production. While for the Marxist liberalism and capitalism are inextricably linked, a liberal operates on the basis that political ideas and structures have a reality separate from the economic.

Another core liberal assumption is that societies are for the benefit of the individual—the common weal is assumed to flow from maximizing individual freedom, whether in the market or in social life. Liberals would reject the notion of formulating overall policies to promote an abstract 'public good' and tailoring individuals to fit. The 1980s have seen economic liberalism in full flood: deregulation and privatization have removed many controls from the economic life of individuals. Yet these new 'freedoms' have been matched by repressive social policies—law-and-order budgets soar, central curricula are imposed upon schools, and welfare recipients are spied upon. We have witnessed the retreat of the State in certain spheres but an inexorable advance in others. However, the purpose of this book is not to analyse this contradiction (or indeed liberalism itself) but to spell out the implications of liberal ideas for policing—to examine the problem how to develop a firmly grounded constitutional police force.

What is the constitutional status of public services, such as health, education, or social services? They are part of the executive arm of government and are not independent. Their actions and decisions can be challenged through legislative or judicial channels—the courts or local and central government. A minister of state is responsible to Parliament for the work of any of these departments. The umbrella under which citizens shelter is the belief that we control the state's power by measuring it against the principles of the rule of law—that we live our lives according to rules that are formally legislated, that there are formal mechanisms to determine the meaning of the rules, and that they are enforced according to natural justice. Did the power purported to be exercised exist in law? Were the proper principles applied in the particular instance? Were the right procedures followed?

But is the rule of law still based on rules? We have seen how police powers are no longer sharply and technically defined but increasingly rely on indeterminate ideas of reasonableness, granting much discretion to the officer. Many public agencies, not just the police, have thrown off the restrictions of narrowly drawn powers and now enjoy broad discretionary powers. But these other agencies are still organized in a hierarchical management structure, usually with very clear departmental objectives—the provision of goods or services, whether education, health, or welfare, to a particular part of the population. At branch, regional, or national level there are both considerable control over policy and actions, and review of performance. Their decisions—whether a refusal to grant supplementary benefit in an individual case or an overall policy on cold-weather payments—are subject to strict administrative review by the courts. In other words, although the broad discretion is on its face contrary to the rule of law, the constitutional status of these agencies is guaranteed by democratic mechanisms and, ultimately, the courts.

As shown in Chapter 7, the police are the one branch of the executive who do not conform to this pattern: they can only be described as a constitutional anomaly. As we have seen, Chief Constables are independent and cannot be instructed how to manage their force. Technically they have no superior minister with direct responsibility to Parliament (although the Home Secretary's influence is far-reaching and represents undoubted power without responsibility). There are few opportunities for MPs to debate or question police policy. The inappropriately named Local Police Authorities have severely restricted operational or financial control. Thus the police operate outside the normal channels for constitutional accountability and possess substantial autonomy. Although they are still subject to the courts, we have seen in decisions such as *Blackburn*[1] that the courts are unwilling to interfere with operational decisions.

Why should we distinguish the police from other public agencies? One reason is that other bodies have clearly defined functions whereas the police have a much more indefinite role in upholding 'law and order'. Unlike other agencies, they are also able to use force, both in making an arrest and in resorting to physical violence when they consider it necessary. This can be paralleled in other areas—although educational authorities do not use physical force they can dictate in detail the movements of children, institute care proceedings and until very recently they could also administer corporal punishment. In 1987 the breadth of welfare powers was shown in the Cleveland child-abuse case where scores of children were taken from their families and put in hospital as possible victims of sexual abuse. But such actions must always be taken for the purposes of 'education', 'welfare', or 'health'. These are terms which can be tested against reasonably precise criteria and find no parallel in the indefinite breadth of purpose of police intervention. These vague powers of intervention in themselves justify the separation of the police from direct political links—governments are not to be permitted such a potent weapon for social control.

These practical implications are one reason to avoid state control of the police and to distinguish them from other public bodies. An allied justification is to be found in the important symbolic role of the police which makes them a touchstone for testing and defining the nature of the constitutional relationship. For the conservative they are an image primarily of order whereby everything and everybody is in its place. Theorists of the right would, following Burke, see a need for deference to a natural authority. The police job is to impose that authority, to educate those lacking deference, and to act in the interests of the established classes.

The liberal image is expressed in terms of law—the police are the embodiment of the law which dictates the limits of power. The concrete protection afforded by the legal system is the yardstick of constitutional health: intervention by the police is closely scrutinized since their actions affect the delicate balance between the freedom of the individual and state power.

Another reason advanced for the anomalous separation of the police from ordinary constitutional mechanisms is that a constable is merely exercising the powers of an ordinary citizen and does not have peculiar rights vested in the office. This theory of the 'citizen in uniform' separates the police from other public agencies. Police functions have been inherent in all theories of citizenship since Anglo-Saxon times. On the other hand, there has never been any 'right' or 'duty' to heal, educate, or minister to one's fellows—health and education authorities have had to be given special powers by legislation to enable them to intervene. Thus there are statutory bodies to which they must account for the exercise of those powers. The police argue that, as citizens, they are accountable to the law like any other citizen and there is no need for further mechanisms. In firing weapons or making arrests, the police officer should be judged according to the same criteria as any citizen.

However, the Granada, the computer, the radio, and the Smith and Wesson make inroads into the picture of the 'citizen in uniform'. Also, as the Stephen Waldorf shooting showed, police officers have to perform their duty where ordinary citizens would be expected to withdraw. In that case, the officers were expected to approach a man they believed to be armed and likely to resist arrest. If constables fail to perform their duty they are liable to prosecution. In the wake of the shooting and of the prosecution of Finch and Jardine, the two detective constables involved, the Police Federation argued that officers should be given immunity from prosecution in such cases.[2] The tests of 'reasonable' force or 'self-defence' necessarily change, depending on whether it is a police officer or a member of the public who is involved.

Under the Police and Criminal Evidence Act 1984, police powers now outnumber those of the citizen, both quantitatively and qualitatively. Nor is it feasible to regard constables solely as individuals, operating in an independent manner and thereby bearing responsibility for their own actions. Practically the officer is in a disciplined, hierarchical force, obliged to obey the lawful commands of senior officers, and cannot be individually responsible for carrying out a particular operation—the parallel now drawn would be the army squaddie.

The indeterminacy of the police powers and functions, their symbolic role, the 'citizen in uniform', all these are arguments to differentiate the police from other public services. Yet we have seen that although there is a multi-faceted system of 'accountability', its very diversity renders it ineffective and there is a need for the operations and policy of the institution as a whole to be made publicly accountable. There is a real problem here: we see the growing power of the police and the covert centralization and political control. The obvious response is to demand standard constitutional accountability. But this immediately encounters a need to separate police from politics. Ministerial responsibility is assumed to involve ministerial control.

The police themselves see their constitutional position as an issue of law—their powers are solely based on law and therefore reviewable by the courts. But this book has frequently demonstrated that the rules that surround policing are discretionary. The legitimacy of police action rests on simple adherence not to rules but to broader standards of fairness: policing is not only rule-based but principle-based. It is this that the police are unwilling to accept. It implies not merely responsibility through the courts but also other forms of democratic/participatory accountability, because accepting that 'good' policing should conform to wider notions of fairness also requires recognition that such standards can only be assessed by bodies representing the community as a whole. An examination of these broad underlying principles—independence, neutrality, and reactivity—as the central elements of constitutional policing may indicate whether it is possible to resolve this dilemma of keeping our police separate from government and yet accountable to the people.

Independence

Independence has been a recurrent theme of this book. The police have always been independent of national political control. This was a concern in the debates over the Metropolitan Police Act, 1829 and the County and Borough Police Act, 1856 and at the time of the 1960 Royal Commission on the Police.

Such independence is not seen as necessary or desirable for other public agencies, even those as closely linked to the criminal justice system as the police. For example, when the Crown Prosecution Service was first suggested in 1981 by the Report of the Royal Commission on Criminal Procedure, it was argued that the system of criminal prosecution should reflect the system of criminal investigation; in other words, the structure should be based on local police areas with a local prosecution authority and the Chief Prosecutor as an independent officer under the Crown. The government's own White Paper rejected this on the grounds that it would encourage local interference in the running of prosecutions. As a result a national (in preference to a local) scheme was introduced under the Prosecution of Offenders Act 1985, whereby local prosecutors are treated as civil servants, responsible to the Director of Public Prosecutions and through the Attorney-General to Parliament.

Can we justify differing structures for criminal investigation and for criminal prosecution? The theoretical benefit is freedom from political control over policing decisions. Police independence should become a check on government, especially when positive rights (of protest or of expression) are not protected by a constitution and the residual rights are fragile ones. Yet the Special Branch raid on the BBC's Glasgow offices in February 1987 (a disturbing parallel to raids on newspaper offices in South Africa), the unlimited resources promised to Chief Constables for policing the miners, or the establishment of the National Reporting Centre all show how easily, under the present system, government wishes can be translated into police action. That action can have many facets—dispersal of gatherings, temporary arrests, searching of persons, vehicles, or houses, seizure of property, surveillance—and their legality is not easily tested in a courtroom.

Few would argue against maintaining the formal separation of the police from government so that no government should have the legal power to order any police operation. Yet political influence is inevitable and this requires some form of political accountability. This could be achieved by extending the province of the Commons' Home Affairs Select Committee to oversee the national and regional development of the police.

But there are also the normal channels of ministerial responsibility. Is there a real contradiction in a minister's answering to Parliament for a police operation, thus providing a forum for debate, and yet not dictating what those operations might be? At present, as was described in Chapter 7, the Home Secretary refuses to answer questions on operational matters, yet under s. 30 of the Police Act 1964 he has the power to require a report on any matter from a Chief Constable. The real paradox is that at the moment he has a statutory right to be informed but does not have to pass the information on to Parliament.

Thus an alternative to a national force with a minister for the police is simply to increase the Home Secretary's responsibility to Parliament—responsibility without power is undoubtedly good for constitutional health. But Parliamentary scrutiny in itself is necessary, given the close links, both through formal meeting and in attitude, that exist between the members of ACPO and the Home Office. But it is insufficient to protect police 'independence' from undue influence. As yet no viable alternative has been proposed to the tripartite system as a means of protecting police independence, but this demands that local police authorities possess genuine authority, counterbalancing that of Chief Constables and the Home Secretary. This does not necessarily include a power to control day-to-day operations but would certainly require the right to specify policy priorities. Other reforms, as suggested earlier, might include the power to appoint senior officers without being restricted to a Home Office short-list; to require reports on events; to lay down policy guidelines; and to exercise real budgetary control.

The Chief Constable is a relic from the days of feudal barons—an 'over-mighty subject', out of the control of constitutional mechanisms. The office has no parallel in Western democracies. To argue for an ideal of police independence is not to seek to entrench this further—rather, by opening up the Home Secretary's role through increased Parliamentary responsibility and by augmenting that of the LPAs, it is to ensure that we attain independence balanced by public interest, defined by democratic procedures.

Neutrality

Any concept of 'fairness' includes neutrality. It is difficult in view of their history to see the police as a neutral institution: both law and society reflect the importance of property rights and the market as well as the dominance of capital over labour. Nor is to be wondered at that the projected image of the police is one not of partiality but of the 'thin blue line', defending an abstract public good from competing interests.

Neutrality is not just about industrial disputes and political demonstrations—the issue arises much more frequently on the street, where police sensitivity to the rights of an individual varies according to his racial, social, and economic traits. In 1985 Commissioner Newman authorized a new police code[3] exhorting officers 'to show compassionate respect for the dignity of the individual and to treat every person of whatever social position, race or creed, with courtesy and understanding'. The rights to privacy and respect remain more in evidence for the middle-class, middle-aged white than for the working class, ethnic groups, and the young. Yet 'fairness' among such groups is a prerequisite to the recognition of police authority.

Countries can legislate to create independence for their police but there is no way of legislating for neutrality—racial discrimination is a disciplinary offence for an officer yet there is no recorded instance in which this regulation has been invoked. On the streets 'cop culture' incorporates strong elements of machismo, sexism, and racialism. It is hostile to 'soft' policing and this in turn deters recruits who might undermine entrenched attitudes. The rejection of the police as a career is especially strong among ethnic communities (although there has been a substantial increase in the recruitment of women and graduates). Basic training has improved but it still has only a temporary liberalizing effect which is soon submerged in the overwhelming ethos of the tough-guy crimefighter.

At present it seems that neutrality must necessarily be imposed from outside. For the individual officer this can only come from senior management—positive recruitment initiatives, longer and more intensive training and social education, active enforcement of the disciplinary code. More powerful police authorities and more zealous parliamentary scrutiny might assist on general policy. But the courts could also contribute by recognizing an obligation to police the police so that they are seen to respect the rights of every suspect.

Reactive Policing

Power is more acceptable where its boundaries are both known and (more importantly) accepted. We require, for instance, clarity in criminal offences or rules for arrest. Throughout this book it has been suggested that although police work is an open-ended occupation its borders are defined by the constraints which we impose—the economic resources available, the technical facilities, and the legal powers. In the 1980s all these constraints have proved a frail barrier to an expanding police role. Resources have consistently been made available to the police for specific campaigns; technical developments in computing have increased the police capacity to maintain records on citizens; weaponry and riot tactics in civil situations have expanded the notions of 'minimum force'; the Police and Criminal Evidence Act has developed police powers and made them even more subjective and discretionary. The Public Order Act 1986 follows a similar path in creating further ill-defined powers and offences.

The constraints have been jettisoned as a result of the neglect of the traditional political convention not to use the criminal justice system directly for governmental purposes—in other words, the convention which recognizes that the government too is bound by the rule of law. The miners' strike in 1984–5 was an unprecedented modern example of direct government interference for political objectives.

What other positive principle might provide adequate boundaries? Perhaps 'fairness' suggests that policing should be reactive—that is, that intervention should occur only in response to the committing of a criminal offence or breach of the peace or the immediate apprehension of one of these. It is a yardstick which reduces the possibility of arbitrary and discriminatory policing and emphasizes two salient characteristics—that policing should be minimal and that it is a public service.

The police reject the notion of limiting their job to what has been pejoratively described as 'fire-brigading'—that is, waiting in the station for trouble and then sallying forth to pour water on the flames. They argue that first and foremost policing involves prevention of crime through informing and educating the public, through the schools and Neighbourhood Watch schemes, as well as by patrolling the streets. Indeed, they have embraced the multi-agency approach to social control, working with the educational, welfare, health, and community sectors, identifying problems and working together to produce informal, non-penal solutions. This can mean intervention in the community on a day-to-day basis, 'community' policing in a wide sense of the phrase. The police would stress the positive aspects of working with youngsters, seeking not to invoke the criminal justice system but integrate police work with the interests of the community and of public agencies. They can be seen as acting in a similar fashion to other service agencies—is this 'improper' policing?

It seems churlish to dismiss such positive approaches but even with strict limits any broad approach to preventive policing carries unacceptable implications for police control over private life. As was argued in Chapter 6, the work of other public agencies can be distinguished—there is a welfare basis to the social worker's or the teacher's involvement in families and schools. By inclination as well as by training, they opt instinctively for non-penal, conciliatory, or therapeutic solutions to the family or social problems they face. An alcoholic will be seen not as an actual or potential offender but as a 'patient' or 'client'. The action taken will primarily be seen as in the interests of the client. (Whether the client sees it in that light is another question.) The policeman's training is oriented quite differently, towards crime and punishment and not towards welfare, nor is there the same professional ethic of confidentiality.

Preventive policing has an immediate analogy with preventive medicine. But, as was argued in Chapter 4, 'crime' has a different social reality to disease. Disease defines itself but the 'problem of crime' is what a society makes it. Preventive approaches involve a reversal of the proper relationship between the police and the community—in 1979 the Chief Constable of Kent, Barry Pain, proposed that the police should, like old-time vicars, be given access to classrooms to run courses in 'citizenship'. The proposal has been partially enacted in the Education Act 1986 but it represents aspirations to a status and function for the police that should be resisted by a liberal society.

The growth of the multi-agency approach, of community, juvenile, and school liaison officers, involves a deeper penetration (and thereby regulation) of civil society than mere beat patrols, although patrolling was introduced in the nineteenth century partly to control the leisure time of the working class. It is an involvement with the minutiae of daily life that is incompatible with the liberal theory of the individual.

This analysis supports the idea that policing should be basically minimal and 'reactive'. An argument put forward against 'reactivity' as a fundamental principle of policing is that it is absurd to wait for a terrorist attack or a serious crime if by judicious surveillance of likely suspects one can prevent them. Prevention of crime has been a byword for the police since Patrick Colquhoun and his Dock Police in the 1790s and is the first duty laid down in the 1985 Metropolitan Force's 'Code of Professional Duties'.

Investigation and prevention are inextricably linked since the investigation of one offence will bring to light other offences, already committed or planned. It would be absurd to suggest that the police should not intervene or take notice of offences until they have taken place, nor does the principle of 'reaction' suggest otherwise. In such circumstances prevention may be a valid objective for the police, but the means by which it is accomplished still require close scrutiny. If no actual harm has as yet been done, the justification for police action needs to be that much greater—the anticipated offence must be deemed serious and likely to occur. Such criteria could justify targeting suspected bank robbers, but hardly soliciting information from schoolchildren or photographing the protesters at Greenham Common.

Constitutional Policing

Liberals are fond of talking about constitutions—written ones are the essence of liberalism, detailing the limits of state power and the freedoms of the subject. The provisions of a constitutional code provide an agenda for debate where the issues, the fundamentals of political organization, are already delineated. Uniquely, we have no written constitution to direct us to these critical issues and no tradition of concern—there are few classes on 'the constitution' in British schools.

A 'constitutional question' tends to emerge obliquely: a specific instance will raise the general issue. The Westlands Helicopter affair in 1986 contained a critical question whether the civil servant had a responsibility to the minister or to Parliament. The 'Zircon spy satellite' affair in 1987 led to questions on the relationship between the Attorney-General and Special Branch. Here there was scope for discussion, but normally the constitutional rules have through history become quite explicit, whether the question is the role of the monarch, the legislative process, or courtroom procedure.

We represent these through symbolic rituals—the state opening of Parliament or a criminal trial. The police, as has been suggested, also have a place in this symbolic universe—'Here comes the Law.' But the Law, when it arrives, is not encumbered with the specific rules and procedures that dictate royal, parliamentary, or courtroom affairs. Police action is tempered with discretion and subjective judgement. The penumbra of their powers is wide, their actions are very visible, and they are a continuing testing ground of the health of social and political freedoms. It has been the thesis of this book that these freedoms are under constant pressure—authority feeds on itself, always seeking greater control. The obscurity of their task and the width of their powers make the police as an institution vulnerable to the authoritarian tendencies in our society.

For this reason we should concern ourselves with the formal constitutional status of the force—protecting its independence and extending its accountability; giving more substance to its much vaunted neutrality; and finally, trying to persuade the police and ourselves that the police should be a final resort where other means of resolution have failed. At the moment the tentacles of the police stretch out to treat people and events as potential policing problems, and crime/punishment takes precedence over other, more welfare-oriented, paradigms. It is the ubiquity of the simplistic 'law 'n order' approach that needs countering, and one technique for doing that is to build a constitutional corral for the office of constable.

Notes and Further Reading

Where there is an abridged reference (author and date only), the full reference will be found in the Bibliography.

Chapter 1

1. *Policy Studies Institute* (1983), p. 78.
2. Hayes, quoted in F. Pearce; *Crimes of the Powerful* (Pluto, 1976).
3. P. Hirst (1975).

Many of the themes touched on here are explored in detail in chapters on crime, public order, etc. For an introduction to authoritarian police systems see B. Chapman (1970). D. Black (1980) is a valuable American sociological study on why people involve the police and how the police deal with situations. There have been several studies of how the police use their time: J. Morgan (1986); R. Tarling and J. Burroughs (1985); *Policy Studies Institute* (1983). The social-service aspects of police work are considered in M. Chatterton (1976). Modern studies of the tactics of policing include J. Alderson (1979) and Lord Scarman (1982).

Chapter 2

1. G. Rusche and O. Kircheimer, *Punishment and Social Structure* (Columbia University Press, 1939), p. 19.
2. E.P. Thompson (1975).
3. D. Hay (1975).
4. I. McDonald, 'The Creation of the British Police', *Race Today* (1973), 5: 11.
5. J. Lyman, 'The Metropolitan Police Act 1829', *Journal of Criminology, Criminal Law and Police Science* (1964), 55: 141.
6. R. Storch (1976).
7. M. Brogden (1981).
8. *Policy Studies Institute* (1983), p. 130.
9. Storch, op. cit., p. 495.
10. T. Bunyan (1977).

11. M. Ignatieff, 'The Police and the People: The Birth of Mr Peel's Blue Locusts', *New Society* (30 Aug. 1979), p. 443.
12. Thompson, op. cit.
13. R. Fosdick, *European Police Systems* (Patterson Smith, 1969) p. 53, quoted in Brogden, op. cit.
14. D. Phillips, 'Riots and Public Order in the Black Country' in R. Quinault and J. Stevenson (eds.), *Popular Protest and Public Order* (Allen and Unwin, 1974).
15. E. Glover, 'The English Police', *Police Chronicle* (1934), p. 62, quoted in Brogden, op. cit.
16. T. A. Critchley (1978), p. 122.
17. R. Geary (1985), ch. 3.
18. K. Coates, *Tom Mann's Memoirs* (1967), p. 220, quoted in Brogden, op. cit.

C. R. Jeffery (1969) gives an account of the Anglo-Saxon and Angevin developments in criminal justice; J. Hall (1952), D. Hay (1975), and E. P. Thompson (1975) are enthralling accounts of eighteenth-century criminal justice. R. Reiner (1985) gives an excellent overview of recent literature on the history of the police themselves. The orthodox history is T. Critchley (1978), and good articles are J. Lyman, art.cit., J. Hart (1955), and R. Storch (1975, 1976).

Chapter 3

1. J. Alderson (1979).
2. S. Manwaring-White (1983).
3. B. Cox *et al.* (1977).
4. Oppressive interrogation also came to light at the trial of those accused of the murder of P.C. Blakelock at Broadwater Farm: a 15-year-old youth had been held for three days clad only in a blanket and underpants, and a youth of 16 but with a mental age of 7 had also been induced to confess.
5. D. Steer (1980).
6. M. Benn and K. Worpole (1986).

The starting-points are the Royal Commission on the Police (1962) and the Royal Commission on Criminal Procedure (1981). R. Reiner (1985) and T. Bunyan (1977) provide overviews of recent developments, as do S. Manwaring-White (1983) and J. Alderson (1979). K. Heal (1985) gathers together several useful Home Office Research Studies. M.E. Jones (1980) provides real insight into the organization of police work. B. Cox (1977) and S. Box (1983) are studies of police corruption. The State Research Bulletin provides much detailed evidence on the changes in the late 1970s, and the

GLC Police Committee has taken over its mantle in the 1980s. There are several guides to the Police and Criminal Evidence Act—I use V. Bevan and K. Lidstone (1985). A critique of the statute can be found in L. Bridges (1983) and L. Christian (1983).

Chapter 4

1. P. Devlin, *The Enforcement of Morals* (Oxford University Press, 1965).
2. B. Whitaker (1979).
3. K. Heal *et al.* (eds.) (1985), ch. 10.
4. M. Benn and K. Worpole (1986).
5. J. Mitford, *The American Prison Business* (Penguin, 1977).
6. R. Clarke and M. Hough (1980).
7. P. Morris (1981).
8. D. Steer (1980).

The Annual Criminal Statistics and the Home Office British Crime Survey (M. Hough (1982)) are the staple diet here. A.K. Bottomley (1973) is still a useful guide to interpretation of the statistics. Chapters 5–10 in K.Heal (1985) are specific studies. R. Grimshaw and T. Jefferson (1987) is a comprehensive study of beat policing. The essays in R. Clarke and M. Hough (1980) are a mine of information, as is the overview by P. Morris (1981) and D. Steer (1980). M. Benn (1986) has a useful section on 'hot pursuit'. S. Box (1983) and J. Reiman, *The Rich Get Richer and the Poor Get Prison* (Wiley, 1979), both provide alternative accounts of the question 'What is crime?'

Chapter 5

1. T. Critchley (1978), pp. 163–5. Also D. Richter, *Riotous Victorians* (1981).
2. R. Geary (1985).
3. R. Stevenson and C. Cook, *The Slump* (Cape, 1977), pp. 161–75 and ch. 12.
4. Geary, op. cit., p. 66.
5. Ibid., p. 104.
6. S. Taylor, 'The Scarman Report and explanations of riots' in J. Benyon (ed.), *Scarman and After* (Pergamon, 1984).
7. C. and L. Tilly (eds.), *Class and Collective Violence* (Sage, 1981); G. Rudé, *The Crowd in History* (Wiley, 1964); E. Hobsbawm, *Primitive Rebels* (Manchester, 1959); E.P. Thompson, op. cit.
8. R. Dworkin, *Taking Rights Seriously* (Duckworth, 1977), p. 194.
9. T. Ward (1986).
10. Scarman (1975).
11. *1985 Annual Report of Metropolitan Police Commissioner.*

12. R. Reiner (1985), p. 203.
13. Rudé, op. cit., p. 255.
14. Geary op. cit., p. 134.
15. Hansard, 12 Feb. 1946, cols. 199–200.

The law on civil liberties might best be read in H. Street (1973). The Public Order Act 1986 is outlined in R. Card (1987). There have been several studies of industrial disputes and inner-city disturbances including J. Coulter (1984); B. Fine (1985); C. Unsworth (1982); M. Kettle (1982); D. Cowell (1982); R. Geary (1985); Lord Scarman (1974 and 1982); M. Jones (1982); and T. Ward (1986).

Chapter 6

1. K. O'Donovan, *Sexual Divisions in Law* (Weidenfeld and Nicholson, 1985), p.181.
2. S. Manwaring-White (1983), ch. 4.
3. Metropolitan Police Commissioner's Strategy Report to the Home Secretary, Jan. 1986.
4. H. Donnison, J. Scola, and P. Thomas, *Neighbourhood Watch: Policing the People* (Libertarian Research, 1986).
5. 1984 Annual Report of Metropolitan Police Commissioner (Cmnd 9541).
6. *London Evening Standard*, 18 Feb. 1987, p. 2, quoting R. Reiser.
7. R. Storch (1976).
8. Anonymous, quoted in R. Reiner (1985), pp. 98–9.
9. *Policy Studies Institute* (1983), vol. iv, ch. iv.
10. S. Jeffreys and J. Radford, 'Contributory Negligence or Being a Woman?' in P. Scraton (ed.), *Causes for Concern* (Pelican, 1984).
11. For a powerful dissection of the link between the moral and the material economies, see David Edgar, 'Bitter Harvest', *New Socialist* (Sept./Oct. 1983), p. 19.
12. H. L. A. Hart, *Law, Liberty and Morality* (Oxford University Press, 1963).

Studies of police surveillance techniques are T. Bunyan (1977) and S. Manwaring-White (1983). H. Donnison, op. cit., is a recent study of the Neighbourhood Watch schemes. The Advisory Council on Police in Schools has produced a report on the subject (1986). The Institute of Race Relations (1979) surveyed police racialism in their evidence to the Royal Commission on Criminal Procedure, but see also R. Reiner (1985) and P. Gordon (1983). S. Box (1983), ch. 4, has a useful introduction to the problems of sexual assault on women.

Chapter 7

1. S. Hall (1978).
2. B. Cox (1977).
3. L. Lustgarten (1986).
4. *Hill* v. *Chief Constable of West Yorks* (1987) 1 All ER 1173.
5. For an account of the rules of admissibility in these circumstances, see *Cross on Evidence* (6th edn., Butterworths, 1985), pp. 427 ff.
6. *Miranda* v. *Arizona* (1966) 348 US 436.
7. C. Mullin, *Error of Judgement* (Chatto and Windus, 1986).
8. *R* v. *Allen* (1977), *Criminal Law Review*, p. 163.
9. *Jeffery* v. *Black* (1978) 1 QB 490.
10. *R* v. *Sang* (1980) AC 402.
11. *R* v. *Metropolitan Police Commissioner, ex parte Blackburn*, No. 3 (1973) QB 241.
12. *R* v. *Chief Constable of Devon and Cornwall, ex parte Central Electricity Generating Board* (1981) 3 WLR 961.
13. *R* v. *Chief Constable of Merseyside, ex parte Levy, The Times Law Report*, 18 Dec. 1985.
14. M. Brogden (1981).
15. Lustgarten, op. cit., pp. 39–41.
16. T. Bunyan (1977).
17. *Fisher* v. *Oldham Corporation* (1930) 2 KB 364.
18. S. Bundred, 'Accountability and the Metropolitan Police' in D. Cowell *et al.* (eds.), *Policing the Riots* (Junction, 1982).
19. I have drawn upon S. Spencer, *Police Authorities During the Miners' Strike* (Cobden Trust, 1986).
20. Yet the Home Secretary is entitled to supply equipment to a force without the consent of the LPA: *R* v. *Secretary of State ex parte Northumbria Police Authority* (1987) 2 All ER 282.
21. Lustgarten, op. cit., pp. 20–2.
22. M. Brogden (1982).
23. T. Critchley (1978).
24. D. Brown, 'Civilian review of complaints against the police' in K. Heal (1985), ch. 13.
25. M. Tuck and P. Southgate, *Ethnic Minorities, Crime and Policing* (Home Office Research Study No. 70, 1981). See also S. Box (1983), pp. 99 ff.

There have been many publications on accountability in the last few years—Lustgarten, op. cit., provides a comprehensive legal account. Also well worth looking at are R. Reiner (1985), ch. 6; T. Jefferson (1984); and R. Baldwin (1982).

Chapter 8

1. *ex parte Blackburn*, loc. cit.
2. *Police Review*, 23 Oct. 1983.
3. Metropolitan Police, *The Principles of Policing and Guidance for Professional Behaviour* (1985).

Bibliography

Advisory Council on Police in Schools, *Policing Schools* (ACPS, 1986)

J. Alderson, *Policing Freedom* (MacDonald and Evans, 1975)

—— *Law and Disorder* (Hamish Hamilton, 1984)

—— and P. Stead (eds.), *The Police We Deserve* (Wolfe, 1973)

D. Ascoli, *The Queen's Peace* (Hamish Hamilton, 1979)

V. Bailey (ed.), *Policing and Punishment in the 19th Century* (Croom Helm, 1981)

R. Baldwin and R. Kinsey, *Police Powers and Politics* (Quartet, 1982)

J. Baxter and L. Koffman (eds.), *Police: The Constitution and the Community* (Professional Books, 1985)

M. Benn and K. Worpole, *Death in the City* (Canary, 1986)

T. Bennett (ed.) *The Future of Policing* (Cropwood Papers 15; Cambridge Institute of Criminology, 1983)

J. Benyon (ed.), *Scarman and After* (Pergamon, 1984)

—— and C. Bourn (eds.), *Police: Powers, Procedures and Proprieties* (Pergamon, 1986)

V. Bevan and K. Lidstone, *The Police and Criminal Evidence Act 1984* (Butterworths, 1985)

D. Black, *The Manners and Customs of the Police* (Academic Press, 1980)

A. K. Bottomley, *Decisions in the Penal Process* (Martin Robertson, 1973)

—— and C. Coleman, *Understanding Crime Rates* (Gower, 1981)

S. Box, *Power, Crime and Mystification* (Tavistock, 1983)

L. Bridges and T. Bunyan, 'The Police and Criminal Evidence Act in Context', *Journal of Law and Society* (1983), 10: 1, p. 85

M. Brogden, 'All Police is Conning Bastards, in B. Fine *et al.* (eds.), *Law, State and Society* (Croom Helm, 1981)

—— *The Police: Autonomy and Consent* (Academic Press, 1982)

T. Bunyan, *The Political Police in Britain* (Quartet, 1977)

J. Burrows and R. Tarling, *Clearing Up Crime* (Home Office Research Study 73, also in K. Heal (1985)

M. Cain, *Society and the Policeman's Role* (Routledge and Kegan Paul, 1973)

—— and S. Sadigh, 'Racism, the Police and Community Policing', *Journal of Law and Society* (1982), 9: 1, p. 87

B. Chapman, *Police State* (Macmillan, 1970)

M. Chatterton, 'Police in Social Control' in M. King (ed.), *Control without Custody* (Cropwood Papers 7, Cambridge Institute of Criminology, 1976)

S. Chibnall, *Law and Order News* (Tavistock, 1977)

L. Christian, *Policing by Coercion* (Pluto, 1983)

R. Clarke and M. Hough, *The Effectiveness of Policing* (Gower, 1980)

—— *Crime and Police Effectiveness* (Home Office Research Study 79, 1984)

J. Coulter, S. Miller, and M. Walker, *State of Siege: Miners' Strike 1984* (Canary, 1984)

D. Cowell, T. Jones, and J. Young (eds.), *Policing the Riots* (Junction, 1982)

B. Cox, J. Shirley, and M. Short, *The Fall of Scotland Yard* (Penguin, 1977)

T. Critchley, *A History of Police in England and Wales* (Constable, 1978)

M. Dummett *et al.*, *Southall 23 April 1979* (NCCL, 1980)

S. Field and P. Southgate, *Public Disorder* (Home Office Research Study 72, 1982)

B. Fine and R. Millar, *Policing the Miners' Strike* (Lawrence and Wishart, 1985)

Sir H. Fisher, *The Confait Case: Report* (HMSO, 1977)

R. Geary, *Policing Industrial Disputes 1883 to 1985* (Cambridge, 1985)

P. Gordon, *White Law* (Pluto, 1983)

M. Grigg, *The Challenor Case* (Penguin, 1965)

R. Grimshaw and T. Jefferson, *Interpreting Police Work* (Allen and Unwin, 1987)

P. Hain (ed.), *Policing the Police* (Calder, 1979)

—— (ed.) *Policing the Police 2* (Calder, 1980)

J. Hall, *Theft, Law and Society* (Bobbs Merrill, 1952)

S. Hall *et al.*, *Policing the Crisis* (Macmillan, 1978)

A. Harrison and J. Gretton (eds.), *Crime UK 1986* (Policy Journals, 1986)

J. Hart, 'Reform of the Borough Police', *English Historical Review* (July 1955)

—— 'Police' in W. Cornish (ed.), *Crime and Law* (Irish University Press, 1978)

D. Hay, 'Property, Authority and the Criminal Law' in D. Hay (ed.), *Albion's Fatal Tree* (Penguin, 1975)

K. Heal (ed.), *Policing Today* (HMSO, 1985)

P. Hirst, 'Marx and Engels on Law, Crime and Morality' in I. Taylor. *et al.* (eds.), *Critical Criminology* (Routledge and Kegan Paul, 1975)

E. Hobsbawm, *Primitive Rebels* (Manchester University Press, 1959)

—— and G. Rudé, *Captain Swing* (Penguin, 1969)

S. Holdaway (ed.), *The British Police* (Edward Arnold, 1979)

—— *Inside the British Police* (Basil Blackwell, 1983)

M. Hough and P. Mayhew, *The British Crime Survey* (Home Office Research Study 76, 1983)

Institute of Race Relations, *Police Against Black People* (IRR, 1979)

T. Jefferson and R. Grimshaw, *Controlling the Constable* (Muller, 1984)

C. R. Jeffery, 'Development of Crime in Early English Society' in W. Chambliss (ed.); *Crime and the Legal Process* (McGraw Hill, 1969)

M. Jones, *Organisational Aspects of Police Behaviour* (Gower, 1980)

—— and J. Winkler, 'Policing in a Riotous City', *Journal of Law and Society* (1982), 9: 1, p. 103

M. Kettle, 'The National Reporting Centre' in B. Fine, op. cit.

—— and L. Hodges, *Uprising!: The Police, the People and the Riots in Britain's Cities* (Pan, 1982)

P. Laurie, *Scotland Yard* (Penguin, 1970)

J. Lea and J. Young, *What Is To Be Done About Law and Order?* (Penguin, 1984)

L. Leigh, *Police Powers* (Butterworths, 1985)

L. Lustgarten, *The Governance of Police* (Sweet and Maxwell, 1986)

S. Manwaring-White, *The Policing Revolution* (Harvester, 1983)

R. Mark, *Policing a Perplexed Society* (Allen and Unwin, 1977)

—— *In the Office of Constable* (Collins, 1978)

G. Marshall, *Police and Government* (Methuen, 1965)

M. Maxfield, *Fear of Crime in England and Wales* (Home Office Research Study 78, 1984)

J. Morgan, 'How Police Use Their Time' in A. Harrison, op. cit.

P. Morris and K. Heal, *Crime Control and the Police* (Home Office Research Study 67, 1981)

D. McBarnet, *Conviction* (Macmillan, 1981)

D. McNee, *McNee's Law* (Collins, 1983)

Policy Studies Institute, *Police and People in London*, 4 vols. (PSI, 1983)

R. Reiner, *The Politics of the Police* (Wheatsheaf, 1985)

Royal Commission on the Police, *Final Report* Cmnd. 1728 (HMSO, 1962)

Royal Commission on Criminal Procedure, *Report* Cmnd. 8092 (HMSO, 1981)

G. Rudé, *The Crowd in History* (Wiley, 1964)

Lord Scarman, *Report of Inquiry into the Red Lion Square Disorders of 15 June 1974* Cmnd. 5919 (HMSO, 1974)

—— *The Scarman Report: The Brixton Disorder 10–12 April 1981* Cmnd 8427 (HMSO, 1981; republished Penguin, 1982)

A. Silver, 'The Demand for Order in Civil Society' in D. Bordua (ed.), *The Police* (Wiley, 1967)

C. Steedman, *Policing the Victorian Community* (Routledge and Kegan Paul, 1984)

D. Steer, *Uncovering Crime* (Royal Commission on Criminal Procedure Research Study 7, HMSO, 1980)

P. Stevens and C. Willis, *Race, Crime and Arrests* (Home Office Research Study 58, 1979)

R. Storch, 'The Plague of Blue Locusts: Police Reform and Popular Resistance in Northern England 1840–57', *International Review of Social History* (1975), p. 20

—— 'The Policeman as Domestic Missionary', *Journal of Social History* (Summer 1976), ix: 4

I. Taylor, *Law and Order: Arguments for Socialism* (Macmillan, 1981)

E.P. Thompson, *Whigs and Hunters* (Penguin, 1975)

M. Tuck and P. Southgate, *Ethnic Minorities, Crime and Policing* (Home Office Research Study 70, 1981)

C. Unsworth, 'The Riots of 1981', *Journal of Law and Society* (1982), 9: 1, p. 63

T. Ward, *Death and Disorder* (Inquest, 1986)

B. Whitaker, *The Police in Society* (Eyre Methuen, 1975)

C. Willis, *The Use, Effectiveness and Impact of Police Stop and Search Powers* (Home Office Research Unit (1983) in K. Heal (1985))

Index